BOYS:
Changing the Classroom, Not the Child

Daniel J Hodgins

Copyright © 2009 by Daniel J Hodgins

All Rights Reserved. No part of this book may be reproduced, copied or utilized in any form or by any means, electronic, mechanical, photocopying, recording, or by any information storage and retrieval system, without permission in writing from the publisher. Inquiries should be addressed to: .

dkj5075@aol.com

Library of Congress Cataloging-in-Publication Data

Hodgins, Daniel J., 1948-
  Boys: changing the classroom, not the child / by Daniel J Hodgins.
      p. cm.
  ISBN 097-8923568948
      1. Boys--Education. 2. Boys--Psychology. 3. Boys--Discipline. 4. School discipline. 5. Classroom management. 6. Academic achievement. I. Title.
  LB1390.H63 2009
  372.1823'41--dc22
                          2009021972

Manufactured in the United States of America

For boys and those who celebrate them

Contents

INTRODUCTION
What About Those Boys? • vii

CHAPTER ONE
Boys Becoming Boys • 1

CHAPTER TWO
Creating a "Boy-Friendly" Environment • 25

CHAPTER THREE
The Curriculum • 39

CHAPTER FOUR
The Hard Parts • 73

CHAPTER FIVE
Success Stories • 91

CHAPTER SIX
Conclusion • 97

Resources • 99

Category Index • 100

Acknowledgments

This book is a collection of wisdom and observations of my thirty-plus years of working with children and families. I feel so honored to have been given an opportunity to gain the many experiences and knowledge that assisted in this project.

So many names and faces passed in front of me—boys and teachers who taught me how to look at children and their many differences that must be celebrated. A number of individuals have mentored and supported my development in creating this book. It would never have happened without them. You know who you are, but just in case, I'd like to thank you:

Leslie and Leonard Lieberman, professors who help me go from my backyard thinking to thinking about the world.

The incredible and gifted teachers at Mott Community College Early Childhood Learning Center in Flint, Michigan, who provided me with countless stories and real life experiences that supported every aspect of this book. Special thanks to Colleen Hames and Valorie Nelson who helped me with the many pictures that celebrated boys.

The children I worked with every day, who made me realize the importance of accepting differences.

Arick, the child who made me a better teacher.

The caring and cooperative early childhood teaching faculty at Mott Community College, who allowed me to be my worse and my best.

My tolerant family, who put up with listening to my ideas, sometimes late in the evening.

My wife, who shared her expertise, as an English teacher, pushing me to make this happen, knowing all along I could do it.

The professional organizations including but not limited to Michigan Association for the Education of Young Children (Mi-AEYC), for the many opportunities to present and gather information from conferences/workshops that assisted in my professional growth.

Thank you all.

Daniel J Hodgins

Introduction: What About Those Boys?

It would be so easy to say that I started to look at boys to help make the educational system more appropriate or to help parents recognize their boys as unique individuals or better yet to make the world a better place for men and women. The reality is that I started to look at boys in a new way when they arrived at my front door to date my daughter! I was shocked as I looked across the room and on the sofa was a "creature" that I didn't recognize, full of characteristics that worried me as a father.

Could all boys be like this? I had been male for more than 30 years and still wasn't prepared for what I saw.

Throughout the following year—also known as the year of *what about those boys?*—I immersed myself in the study of boys and their make-up. The following questions need to be considered:

- Why aren't boys succeeding?
- Why are so many boys being retained?
- Why are so many boys in trouble?

Parents, guardians, and teachers all over the world are asking questions like these.

It was during this time that I began to challenge what I had learned in my education courses, my practices as a teacher of young children, and my parenting ability. How could I have not known that boys are so different from girls? What started out as a way to rescue my daughter now became an intense drive to help parents and teachers understand the different needs of boys and how to support them.

BOYS IN TROUBLE

Observation of children had always been a major part of what I did as a teacher in my early childhood experiences. The observations I made became the implemented curriculum and environmental strategies used daily. The difference now became my intense interest in how boys and girls interacted differently in early childhood settings. In the classroom that I worked in and the many classrooms that I visited across the country I observed some startling differences:

- Boys were expelled more often than girls

- Boys were more likely to be diagnosed with a learning disability
- Boys were more likely to be on medication for ADHD
- Boys were more likely to be sitting in "time-out"

Looking at the research on boys, it seems to conclude similar findings. Boys are in trouble and need our support.

Like many other parents, teachers, and community members, I can no longer ignore the mounting evidence that boys and girls have been "wired" differently and need different kinds of attention from adults. Years of observation and "hands-on" experience as a teacher have convinced me that our practices need to reflect a new understanding of the differences between boys and girls.

What you'll find in this book

As we look at nature and the nurturing of boys, we'll discover the simple bottom line: as teacher and parents, we have to change. The following chapters are about what I know, what I have done, and what I plan to do in the future to help boys become the unique individuals they deserve to be.

Chapter 1 of this book suggests that boys are "wired" differently than girls, and that this has important implications for parents and educators. The results are clear that boys are falling behind girls in most areas.

The development of boys is not only a biological process but also a social one. The observations I have made reflect on these differences. Starting with how boys complete tasks. A simple task like washing his hands can take much longer for boys because of the multiple steps involved and the many distractions that occur around him. This often translates to boys not noticing the details essential for doing many tasks in our early childhood settings.

Feelings seem to be demonstrated differently in boys then girls. This presents challenges with developing empathy and other caring behaviors.

It has been reported that some boys may be 12-18 months developmentally different then girls. If this is true, then boys often act their "stage" in the classroom rather then their chronological age. Is this the reason so many boys are in special education settings?

In almost all of my observations teachers reported that boys seem to lag behind girls in language development. This difference can often be seen in communication patterns, listening skills and writing abilities.

With too much sensory stimulation the boy might go into pause state for protection. There is a fine line between how much is too much stimulation for boys to handle in the classroom.

The development of boys is not only a biological process but is also influenced by culture. This chapter concludes with the interplay of these factors, with an emphasis on the role of cultural conditioning.

Chapter 2 presents ways to create a boy-friendly climate, focusing on strategies for structuring the physical environment we provide for children. Here you'll find suggestions for encouraging active play by providing spaces for running, climbing, water play, digging, roughhousing and solitary activity. All of these environments can help to meet the special interests of boys.

Chapter 3 presents ways to drive the curriculum, especially where boys' development is concerned. Look here for activities that encourage art, movement, outdoor play, songs and music, reading, writing, math, science as a way to explore the world experiences. Finally are computers good or bad? This chapter will lead you to fun, boisterous activities and suggestions for making your classroom come alive for boys.

Chapter 4 is about the "hard parts." It is structured around the tough questions that people ask me as they respond to the challenges posed by preschool boys. How do I help the aggressive boy? What about bullying? How can I avoid power struggles? Are time-outs effective? How can I handle boys roughhousing? Does gunplay and swordfighting create violence? What can I do about superhero play? Boys never want to listen. How can I change that? How does attachment form in boys? Finally do we need to provide same gender classrooms in early childhood education?

Are boys going to make it in our classrooms? Chapter 5 provides some success stories involving boys and educators who acted in ways that are consistent with the spirit of this book.

A sense of belonging is the ultimate goal for both boys and girls in our early childhood settings. Chapter 6, the conclusion, discusses the need for every child to be placed in a climate that supports the emotional well being of children.

The following pages are filled with practical suggestions for teaching boys that have been put to test in my classroom and in many classrooms that I've visited. It is true that girls might be able to benefit from many of the strategies and insights offered here. As my travels take me to far corners of the world to present workshops, I find that most of the questions asked by early childhood educator's focus on boys. It is with this in mind that I've written a book about the differences between boys and girls and practices that support boys in preschool settings. I hope that this book meets your needs.

1 Boys Becoming Boys

New research about brain-based differences between boys and girls is emerging every year. Some of the findings are contradictory. Researchers disagree about their practical implications. This is just what we can expect from such a "hot" area of scientific research. The subject of brain-mediated differences between boys and girls is one of the most controversial issues of the last fifty years, and it will generate debate for at least another fifty years.

As parents and educators, however, we don't have the luxury of waiting for scientists to gather new data and refine their conclusions. We have boys in our lives right now that demand our caring attention today. Therefore it is *not* my purpose in this book to offer a comprehensive scientific theory about the genetic and culturally based differences between boys and girls. My statements about these differences do not apply to *all* boys but rather to large segments of them that populate our early childhood settings. *My aim is simply to offer practical suggestions that you can use immediately* to transform your relationship with boys and create an environment that nurtures them.

With this disclaimer in mind, I suggest that it's useful to act on the hypothesis that boys' brains can be wired in unique ways. Thinking in this way opens up a whole host of new possibilities that can help us "get though" to the kids in our lives. The rest of this chapter singles out a few of these possibilities and then explores ways that you can work effectively with them.

BOYS GO INTO "PAUSE STATE" AFTER COMPLETING TASKS

Arick, who is three and half, goes over to Rebecca, who is four years of age. She is in the puzzle area in a preschool classroom. He grabs a puzzle that she is completing and hits her in the arm. Rebecca's brain tells her to cry first and then yell, "Teacher, teacher!"

The teacher comes over to address the situation and Rebecca says, "Arick hit me."

At this point, the following conversation takes place:

"Remember Arick, we don't hit our friends in school," says the teacher. "How would you like it if Rebecca hit you?"

In response, Arick gives the universal boy gesture: He lifts his shoulders and says, "I don't know."

The teacher says to him, "I want you to sit in the time-out chair and think about your hitting."

The teacher places Arick in the time-out chair. He sits there for about four minutes.

My observation and research can tell you that, while he was in the time-out chair, Arick did not think about hitting Rebecca. If anything, he was hoping that a child would come close enough to the chair so that he could trip her. As soon as Arick hit, his brain went into a "pause state." Anything else that occurred immediately following that task was ignored. In the above example, Arick wasn't listening to the teacher because he was "at pause." Therefore, the strategy used by the teacher was wasted.

I have observed many examples of boys' pause states. One involved a boy in the art area of a preschool classroom. Armed with a full bottle of glue, he was trying to complete an activity the teacher provided that day called "collaging." A small piece of paper was on the table before him, along with many objects for him to attach to his paper with the glue.

As this boy started to glue, his facial expression took on a new intensity. His tongue stuck out and went to the right side of his mouth. Then his hips started to move in a swirling motion, just like the glue that he was squeezing from the bottle onto the paper.

The teacher asked, "Don't you have enough glue?"

The boy ignored the teacher's questions and continued squeezing glue on the paper.

The teacher asked again, "Don't you have *enough* glue?"

Again the boy ignored the teacher.

This continued until the boy emptied all of the glue from the bottle. He stood back and smiled.

The teacher then pointed to all of the choices of objects on the table and asked, "Would you like to put some of these things on your glue?"

The boy was still engaged in looking at his pile of glue. He did not respond to the question.

Finally the teacher started putting things on the boy's pile of glue. In response, he picked up a large pile of buttons, dropped them on the glue, and walked away.

If you ask boys and girls to perform a task such as gluing, you'll probably find that most of the girls will smile and be eager to comply. Boys, however, will often show a puzzled look, grab the glue bottle, and start squeezing without any plan in mind.

This might explain why males are less likely to complete a number of tasks at once and are often more distracted in their thinking. The boy with the glue could only think about gluing—not about how much glue he was using or whether he wanted to "put things" on his glue. For him, in that moment, there was just gluing. When he finished, he went into pause state and ignored the teacher's further suggestions. Perhaps he was hoping for more glue!

Another example of pause state involves the "simple" task of washing hands before snack. This activity includes many steps—and many opportunities for a boy's brain to pause:

1. Turn on Water (play in it)
   Pause

2. Put on Soap (usually too much)
   Pause

3. Rinse Water Off (play in it again)
   Pause

4. Turn Water Off
   Pause

5. Dry Hands (usually on pants)
   Pause

A boy washing his hands might go through five pause states. No wonder it takes him so long!

I have observed that as he matures, a boy can do more tasks before his brain goes into pause state. In addition, the length of time *during* the pause decreases. I also have observed that the more physical activity the boy is involved in after completing the task, the less likely the pause state will continue. Before you spend time talking to a boy regarding some behavior you wish to change, remember to move a boy's brain from pause state to active state. Engage him in a simple physical activity that "wakes up" his brain.

BOYS PROCESS FEELINGS DIFFERENTLY THAN GIRLS

A song that is commonly song in preschool classrooms around the country is

Friends:

Friends, friends, one, two three

All my friends are here with me.

You're my friend; you're my friend,

[as children point to each other]

You're my friend, you're my friend.

Friends, friends, one, two, three

All my friends are here with me.

I am not sure that boys believe this song. Their brains see "intruders," not "friends." Many times boys don't recognize feelings. Talking and singing about feelings doesn't always seem to increase awareness of them.

When four-year-old Sara hits Carol in a preschool classroom and Carol cries, Sara's brain begins to work on the cognitive side first, *Why is she crying?* Then the emotional side kicks in, *Did my hitting cause her to cry? If so, I don't want to hit her anymore.*

When John hits Carol, events unfold in a different way. Carol starts to cry. John watches for a while and then hits her again. His brain is wondering, *Why she is crying?* At that moment, he actually doesn't realize that it might have been due to his hitting her.

In general, early childhood professionals will respond to a situation like this by taking John aside and saying, "We don't hit our friends. Say you're sorry." John usually apologizes, but his brain doesn't understand the concept and soon he will hit again.

PAUSE STATE TO ACTIVE STATE

The following activities seem to move the brain from pause state to active state:

- Getting the boy to shout loudly
- Providing for spinning activities
- Jumping up and down
- Running in place
- Getting the boy to put his hands out in front of him and make loud clapping movements
- Marching legs high
- Putting hands together and pushing on each other with force
- Taking giant steps
- Stretching arms up high

A better practice is to say: "John, you like to hit. Let me find something that you can hit hard." Take him over to a large refrigerator box and let him pound it. Then say, "I can't let you hit Carol, but you can hit this box."

Also remember that acting out feelings seems to develop not only a better understanding of feelings but creates empathy. Asking a boy to run and get a "bag of ice" to put on Carol's bruise seems to help him recognize the importance of helping rather than hurting.

About the time that they reach age two, boys enter full force the drama of what their culture expects of them. It is essential that preschool teachers recognize that boys are saying, *we are different than girls and that is okay*. Boys demonstrate empathy and feeling in their own way. Through modeling, they can learn how to become more sensitive to others. However, they are wired biologically to process their feelings and react to emotions in a "boy-like" manner. Even though boys don't talk about their feelings, they still need opportunities to express them. Role playing with puppets; acting out stories; kicking boxes when angry are all part of the expression they need.

Other observations I have made indicate boys process feelings in ways that differ from girls—for example:

- Boys often release feelings in quick bursts of energy. They might "fly off the handle," yelling *"I hate your guts!"* while stamping their feet. A boy needs a teacher who helps other children get out of his way and provides a space for him to scream if he needs to.

- Sometimes it takes longer for a boy to solve problems that involve emotions. He might not realize that there is a problem, or he might not want to talk about it. A boy will sometimes run under the table, especially if someone is going to force him to talk about his feelings. Give him the space and time he needs. What boys are looking for is someone who says with their actions: *I am here, if you need me.*

- Throwing blocks or toys is sometimes what boys do to express their feelings. Make sure they have things to throw and a target to throw them at. The worst thing to say as a teacher is, "We don't throw blocks at our school." He knows that. Telling him what he can throw is more productive, "I have these balls for you to throw at this wall."

Keeping these points in mind can help us respond more effectively when boys seem to hit and push without remorse. Boys are not "meaner" than girls. They often just don't connect their feelings with their actions.

Boys see the whole more than the details

In a preschool classroom, a teacher was sitting with a group of three to five year-olds. In this gathering were a mixture of girls and boys all anxiously waiting to hear the story she was about to read. Going through the story, the teacher paused to ask questions of the children. The girls leaned forward and responded with lots of statements reflecting details of the pictures they were looking at. The teacher asked them about the next picture, which was a picture of a cougar that drew the boys, who were not usually looking at the book, into the story.

One boy yelled "grrrrrr" then, another boy got on all fours and also started to "grrrrr" until soon all the boys were crawling and roaring like cougars.

The teacher responded, "Stop! We are not playing cougar now. It is story time." It was the only detail the boys' brains noticed, and they were being asked to ignore it.

This teacher isn't alone in her approach to boys who growl like cougars. She is responding the way that educators traditionally do when gathered with boys and girls during story reading or other relatively subdued experiences.

It is no surprise that the girls who saw the picture of the cougar pointed out the color of its fur, the way that the cougar showed its teeth, and other details shown in the picture. The boys saw the cougar as a whole, vividly imagining how such an animal would sound and move if it suddenly leapt into the classroom. Their minds went straight to growling and prowling.

To help boys see the details in the picture of the cougar, the teacher could ask:

- "Tell me how the cougar sounds."
- "What are some parts of the cougar's body?"
- "When does the cougar growl, when he is hungry, sleepy, or all the time?"

Consider another example, which is related to a different activity. Teachers who take preschool boys into the bathroom to wash their hands may notice how many of them hurry to get it done. In addition, the boys might forget to use soap, play in the water longer then you want them to, and leave the room with dripping wet hands. (If the boys *do* bother to dry their hands, they'll probably skip the towels and slap their hands on their pants instead.) A "simple" task of hand washing includes a series of steps—details that the boy's brain glosses over. His focus is on the experience of hand washing as a whole, or on the next anticipated activity.

How many times have you said to boys: "Walk!" "Use your inside voice!" "Flush the toilet!" You might give these directions repeatedly and still not get the expected results. You can do several things to help boys focus on the details involved in following such instructions:

- Repeat activities. Boys' brains need plenty of practice in viewing and responding to details. For example, have them park play cars and trucks in spaces that are labeled for cars and trucks, when they finish. Getting those cars and trucks out to play with is a simple task. Putting them back in their parking spaces is much more complex and challenging. Providing boys practice at putting the cars and trucks in their parking spaces is an important function. It doesn't connect to the brain the first time or sometimes even the fifth time. With practice the brain will see the detail of putting things away.

- Provide visual cues. For example, create a picture of a boy flushing the toilet and tape this picture to the toilet tank.

Additional examples of visual cues for boys include:

- Pictures of children walking—an alternative to the verbal instruction "Use your walking feet."

- Pictures of children covering their ears—an alternative to the verbal instruction "Don't get too loud in here."

- Using dots on a poster to illustrate the passage of time; start with five dots, then four dots, and continue until you get down to one—an alternative to saying "Five more minutes until clean up time."

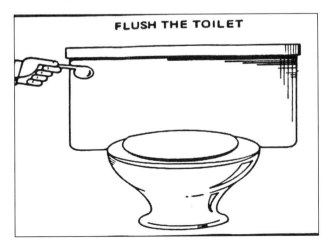

Boys' developmental age can differ from their chronological age

In my travels from classroom to classroom, teachers often report that girls exceed boys in most areas of development. A teacher who works with four-year-old children in a classroom might actually be in the midst of a group with developmental stages that range from two to five.

I'm also not surprised when teachers report that the boys are more challenging than the girls. Remember that a toddler's philosophy of life is, *If you are in my way, I will push you.* When boys are close to the toddler stage of development, we'll see lots of pushing, grabbing, and chasing in a preschool classroom.

As parents and teachers we need to ask: Are we using appropriate strategies in the classroom for children's developmental levels? Are we using assessments based on children's developmental stage rather than their chronological age? Often we don't use assessments that measure the developmental levels of boys.

Our special education classrooms are filled with boys. Many of them are mislabeled as learning disabled or attention deficient. In reality, boys may be acting appropriately for their stage of development. Perhaps boys truly are meeting a classroom expectation to *act your age.*

Boys develop language in visual and kinesthetic ways

Preschool teachers are telling me that boys *and* girls are coming to school with fewer and fewer words. Perhaps this increase is a result of loss of family rituals.

Can you remember when you went on car trips with your family and played I Spy, Slug Bug, or games that involved spotting license plates? Maybe you also played the Name the States and other games that required you to recite a list of facts from memory. All these are family rituals that double as strategies for language development.

Consider another example. While growing up, how many times did you dry the dishes with your siblings or other family members? You probably passed the time during this task by talking to your brothers or sisters about the happenings of the day. This, too, was a powerful way for you to develop your language skills.

Today, many parents and guardians take a different approach. They pop a movie into a DVD player to keep children quiet for as long as possible. When parents *do* talk with their children, most of this time is often devoted to adults giving directions rather than children talking.

Consider this example of Jessica, age four, and her mother during dinner.

Jessica's mother said, "You cannot go swimming for an hour after you eat, because you might get cramps."

Jessica asked, "What is *cramps*?"

That made *cramp* a rare word for Jessica. Her mother explained the meaning.

When Jessica came to school the next day she made statements such as these: "I'm going to have snack, I have cramps." "Let me do some art today, I have cramps." "I'm going to swing, I have cramps." Obviously, Jessica did not always speak the word in the correct context. However, she used the word *cramp* frequently, eventually mastering its correct meaning.

Like Jessica, many girls start using rare words almost immediately. In contrast, boys typically used such a word only when it connected to an action, or when it was associated with a picture or photo.

In addition, girls often use words to describe feelings, while boys prefer to describe actions. My observations of language development in boys indicate that many of them are visual and kinesthetic learners. They readily learn words that relate to running, hopping and crawling. If they can't see it or move it, then it doesn't exist!

Taylor, a boy in a preschool classroom, drew a picture of a girl in the army.

I asked Taylor, "Does your picture have a story?"

"Yes," he said. "It is a girl standing at attention." (Notice that a line attaches the legs.)

I asked, "How will she move?"

"The sergeant will say *at ease* and she then will run a lot," said Taylor. He is developing language with words that connect to action.

The same is true of Sam, age four. He drew a picture of a pregnant woman who is swimming. Notice the number of arms and legs he included to demonstrate the stroking of the arms and the kicking of the legs.

I asked Sam, "Does your picture have a story?"

His response, "Yes, it is a woman who is having a baby, who likes to swim."

I then asked, "What about the baby?"

"Heck! It slows her down," Sam replied.

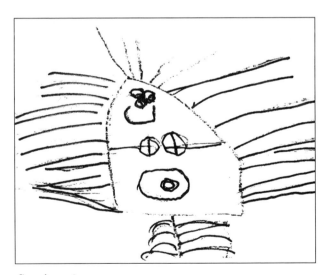

Sam's swimmer

Taylor's "girl in the army"

Boys also latch on to words that relate to bodily functions—especially those from the waist down. CJ, when he was age eight, sang this song:

> *Yankee Doodle,*
> *Went to town*
> *A riding on a spider*
> *Stuck an apple up his butt*
> *And peed apple cider.*

CJ is demonstrating his verbal skills with language that puts words to rhythm and beat.

Earlier in this chapter I mentioned the Friend Song that is sung in many classrooms. In one preschool classroom that I visited, the teacher sang this song with the children. When she was finished, Brent said, "I know this song with different words."

The teacher, wanting to encourage children's language development, responded, "You tell me the words and I will write them down on this poster so we can all sing it."

Brent smiled and dictated the following:

> *Boogers, boogers, one, two three*
> *All my boogers are here with me*
> *Here's one booger, here's one booger*
> *Here's one booger, here's one booger*
> *Boogers, boogers, one, two, three*
> *All my boogers are here with me.*

Is Brent developing language? You bet! Fortunately he was in a classroom where the teacher recognized that Boogers could be more relevant (and more readily demonstrated) than Friends.

In the same spirit, Chapter 3 of this book offers suggestions for songs, finger plays, and chants that can help boys in their quest to master language.

BOYS EXPERIENCE SENSORY OVERLOAD

I had the opportunity to visit a preschool classroom that was well recognized in the community. As I walked in the door, music began to play in the background automatically. Near the entrance was a fish tank that was almost the whole wall length. Colorful posters were hanging on the wall depicting pictures of children from around the world. A large mobile hung over the sign-in desk of paper mache whales.

When I reached a classroom, I immediately noticed that the walls were covered with posters that included shapes, numbers, and colors. There were ten centers set up for children, each with a different carpet color to designate boundaries. Each center included lots of toys and activities that offered choices for children. And from the ceiling hung mobiles the children had made out of pieces of wood and other materials. The teacher was concerned because the boys in her classroom didn't seem to spend much time at activities in the centers.

Contrast this situation with the example of Abdul, a child in another preschool. When his teacher started to limit the number of activities and center choices available to the children, she also limited distractions. Abdul began to stay longer with the activity and focus more on the experience.

When too many options are present in a classroom, some boys can become overly stimulated. This is why some boys in a preschool center become "floaters," going from one center activity to another without long periods of engagement. All that color, texture and visual stimuli say to the boy's brain: *run away, avoid making choices, withdraw,* or *detach.*

In contrast, girls' brains often seem to tolerate a variety of stimulation. The girls' brains are telling them that the lesson is interesting, while the boys' brains are busy wondering when something will happen to break the tedium.

Many preschool settings include "centers," areas for specific types of activity relating to house, art, small toys, and blocks. Other centers—such as those for science, books, writing, water, or music—are usually integrated within those four centers.

I suggest that sometimes you might limit not only the number of center choices but also the number of activity choices within each center. My observation of boys' play indicates that their brains can handle up to four choices of activities at one time. More than four choices often lead to "floating." Rather then providing ten different puzzles for boys to select from in the small toy center, put out multiple copies of only four different puzzles. For boys, "more" is not necessarily better.

You can use additional strategies to prevent overload.

Avoid visual over stimulation

Preschool teachers often are taught to make their classrooms visually pleasing. Through this effort we sometimes create classrooms that have a negative effect on boys' behavior. A classroom that presents too many visual cues can promote distractibility in boys.

Preschool teachers are collectors. We save everything. After all, we never know when we just might be able to use those popsicle sticks and cardboard toilet rolls for a classroom activity. I hardly made it to school on time when the route I took was scheduled for garbage collection. People throw out good stuff—just perfect for my classroom! Like me, other teachers smuggle these treasures into our classrooms and wait for the day to use them. However, all that stuff can be too much for boys.

Boys often need an opportunity to take a visual rest. Without it, boys can have a hard time sorting out details. With this in mind, take a look at wall coverings in your classroom. Allow blank spaces. Avoid covering every spot with posters, signs, art samples, or alphabet letters. Put what is not currently being used into labeled and enclosed bins, out of sight.

In particular, you may find that it helps to use solid-colored carpeting in a classroom. This is less stimulating than carpeting with images of the alphabet, shapes, numbers, or world maps. Teachers have reported to me that when they use solid color carpeting for group activities, the boys seem calmer and do less roughhousing.

The bottom line is simplicity: keeping a classroom visually pleasing means keeping it simple. Keep the room organized, and keep it free from clutter.

Monitor odors

We live in a culture that celebrates artificial odors—scented lighting, plug-in room deodorizers, and extracts added to children's paint and clay. Different types of odors seem to stimulate different parts of the brain. Boys and girls seem to respond differently to such variety. Too often odors can create a pause state in boys.

In one preschool classroom I observed, the teacher decided to add peppermint extract—a highly stimulating odor—to the play dough. Anyone who walked into the room noticed the odor immediately. This created a visible change: The boys ran around and yelled more often. They seemed to have a difficult time focusing on activities. What seemed to be a fun and creative addition to the play dough actually stimulated a rumpus.

I have never had a preschool child ask me to add peppermint to play dough. What children want to do is simply play with the play dough using a variety of instruments.

This does not mean that teachers should avoid stimulating a sense of smell. We simply need to restrain ourselves from adding too much. My rule of thumb is: If you walk into the classroom and find that the smell that you placed in the play dough is what you first notice, then it is too much.

Boys are Wired for Assertiveness

Tommy, a child in my preschool classroom, would take a broom handle, wrap it around his waist with duct tape, and then ask, "Do you see any ducks?" He was playing Duck Hunting, imitating his father, a duck hunter. The other children would get annoyed at Tommy, who asked this question repeatedly.

They would point to the climber and yell, "Yes, there are three over there." Tommy would run smiling with his pretend gun and try and shoot the pretend ducks.

Some teachers would describe Tommy's behavior as violent. Yet there is a difference between violence and assertiveness. Violence is learned, while assertiveness is wired into boys.

Testosterone seems to be present in boys in higher levels than in girls. This is the hormone that supports the many physical, risk-taking behaviors that we see in boys—including running, jumping, climbing and hitting—that sometimes border on dangerous. A preschool boy often displays more "spikes" of testosterone levels during the day then girls.

Assertiveness that might be linked to these changes in testosterone is visible in any preschool classroom. From my own teaching experience, I have images of Charles and Dominique chasing other boys, who are the "robbers." They catch them and lock them up to protect the world. Jacob and Sam are building a rocket ship out of blocks to go after the bad guys and protect the Universe. Wayne is building a tower that reaches higher than his eyes, only to knock it over while he screams, "Look out below!"

The quantity and kind of assertive behaviors in boys always depends on their age and how they have been taught to direct their energy. Boys as young as four and five are being labeled attention deficit hyperactive disorder (ADHD) when in reality they might simply be active, bored, and highly intelligent. A combination of these factors often get boys in trouble.

To help boys cope with testosterone spikes, you can provide a variety of activities that support the need for physical movement in the classroom and that takes into account the differences between boys and girls. Chapter 3 of this book offers detailed suggestions.

Boyhood in Our Culture

When my daughter was about age three, she decided to only wear dresses to preschool. She was fond of twirling around, singing and prancing, and acting just like a little princess.

My wife and I were puzzled. We were progressive parents, aiming to make sure that our daughter was raised without gender stereotypes. We encouraged her to play with trucks and ambulances. We read books to her that showed girls climbing in trees. We did house chores together without describing them as traditionally male or female.

In light of all this, I was flabbergasted by my daughter's "girl" behavior. Where was it coming from? After a period of reading and reflecting on my experiences as a parent and educator, I concluded that our daughter was simply acting on a host of messages that she received from birth.

Early in childhood, children begin to work out for themselves what it means to be a boy or a girl. By age five, most children have learned the gender roles that a society assigns to its members. I saw this in my own classroom, where I often observed preschool girls going through a pink and frilly phase and preschool boys spending their days imitating superheroes. Girls spent more of their time in the dress-up or kitchen center of their preschool classroom. Boys engaged in activities that made them feel powerful, such as constructing block towers and knocking them down with a toy truck.

In many cases, these phases pass. Still, I observed that boys more often end up in school offices for discipline challenges than girls. Boys are more likely to be placed in special education classes and in programs for children with delayed speech and language.

Are these events due to biological differences or cultural messages—"nature" or "nurture"? This is no longer the operating question. Research reveals that the development of boys and girls results from a complicated interaction of biology *and* society. "Nature" and "nurture" interact in a dance that we are only starting to understand.

It is my intention in this book to address both sides of the equation.

PARENTS SEND MESSAGES ABOUT WHAT "REAL BOYS" DO

During hospital play, Mindy was pretending to give Josette a shot. Mindy said, "I will give you this shot and it will make you feel better."

After the shot was administered, Josette said, "I feel a lot better now, Doctor."

Mindy responded, "I am not a doctor. I am a nurse. Only boys can be doctors."

Mindy has definite ideas about gender roles even though her mother is a doctor. Messages about what is appropriate based on gender are so strong that even when children are exposed to different attitudes and experiences, they will revert back to stereotyped choices. This helps to explain conversations like the one above.

Simple imitation plays a large role in helping children learn about what boys and girls are supposed to do. Children who watch their mother do the dishes many times may conclude that doing the dishes is a female activity. They may also hear fathers say, "I'll fix the car—that's not your mom's job."

In addition, parents and guardians are not always aware of how much we subtly reinforce gender stereotyping through our compliments. Examples include our comments on how pretty a little girl looks in her dress or how big a little boy looks in his jeans and shirt.

Parents and guardians also teach boys and girls about gender by actively rewarding some behaviors and punishing others. Adults might praise girls—and discourage boys—for doing the same activity. A mother might praise her daughter when the child picks some flowers from the garden and rushes into the house to present the beautiful bouquet. Yet the same mother might express anger with her son who picks the flowers and runs into the house to present her with the bouquet—roots, dirt, and all. In our preschool setting, I noticed that the parents and guardians who volunteered would praise girls more frequently than boys. Praise would include "That is a pretty picture"; "I like it when you eat your snack all up"; and "good girl." Boys, however, were often corrected: "Sit down in that chair"; "Stop running, you could fall"; and "Use your softer voice." These practices reinforce gender stereotypes.

Behind such overt behaviors in parents and guardians are deep seated and unconscious beliefs about gender roles. These beliefs can color our daily interactions with children in profound ways. The girls in my preschool setting—more frequently than the boys—were hugged and kissed by the parents and guardians who came to pick them up at the end of the day. Girls were more often asked, "How was your day?" In contrast, boys more often got help to gather items in their backpacks, more often got instructions to tie their shoes, and were more often bribed to leave preschool without making a fuss. Boys were often subtly encouraged to take risks, become independent, and assert authority.

Fathers, I have observed, become particularly anxious when their sons fail to conform to gender stereotypes and will take steps to limit unconventional behavior. One father in my preschool setting voiced concern about his boy wearing a ballerina dress in the classroom. This happened even though his boy, wearing the dress, was playing a superhero character that was out to save the world. While volunteering in the classroom, another father said to his son, "David, boys don't color their fingernails" (David was using colored markers to color his fingernails at the art area). Even the most progressive fathers can become uncomfortable when they see their sons playing with dolls or doing other traditional "girl activities."

Of course, parenting alone does not define why boys more often want to run, why boys are having difficulty in school, and why boys more often bully each other. Yet we need to take parental influences into account as we think about new ways to create classroom climates that help boys reach their full potential.

This is a letter that I send home to parents/guardians at the beginning of each year to help celebrate boys' differences.

September 9, 2009

Dear Parents,

Below is a list of what your sons may bring home this year.

- A pirate song
- Chickenpox
- All black, brown or purple paintings
- A bite mark
- Things in their pocket
- A string around their neck that used to have cereal on it
- Words you don't want to hear
- Something he wrote that you cannot read
- Something in a baggy that you can't recognize
- Pushing
- "I can do it"
- Lots of glue on something

Everything he does is an essential part of his growth!

Sincerely yours,

Dan Hodgins

TELEVISION AND OTHER MEDIA SEND MESSAGES ABOUT GENDER

During a day in his preschool, Joshua started to throw chairs in a casual fashion. Soon after he started, Teddy joined in the play. Within minutes two other boys got in on the game. I watched this play for about 10 minutes, noticing that the underlying intention was not to hurt anyone. In fact, the play really didn't seem to have any purpose at all.

I went up and asked the boys, "Hey guys, what are you up to?"

They responded, "We are playing *Jerry Springer*."

I was shocked. Is it possible that four- and five-year-olds were watching *Jerry Springer?* I then asked, "Do they throw chairs on *Jerry Springer?*"

They all yelled, "Just before they fight, they throw the chairs."

Sure enough, they all had been watching *The Jerry Springer Show* and were acting out the part that was most relevant to them—throwing chairs.

During my next informational meeting for parents and guardians, I discussed the subject of television viewing. Most of the adults believed that children didn't really pick up information from television, especially as it relates to gender roles, and said that television was used more as a pre-dinner babysitter. In response, I became a careful reporter, sharing my observations about what their children were playing and how that might be influenced by their TV viewing.

Television, movies, and printed media all encourage boys and girls to develop and maintain gender stereotypes. The next time you watch a commercial on television with messages about a product's strengths, notice whose voice of authority is doing the talking—male or female?

Television and movies often show images that spotlight women's beauty and men's strength. When reviewing movies, for example, I repeatedly saw girls portrayed as feminine and pretty, and often needing to be rescued by boys. In contrast, boys are strong and seldom express emotions. Boys watching television notice that it's the man's job to do repairs, exercise power, and in general make things happen. Over the last few decades, powerful images have taught boys that:

- The Maytag Man can fix anything.
- Mr. Clean can do it all.
- If you want to be a strong cowboy, then smoke Camels.
- Wearing the right kind of underwear can make you toss a ball like Michael Jordan.
- Eating spinach can make you like Popeye—"Strong to the finish."

In magazines, men are very seldom portrayed doing housework. Instead, they are likely to be shown outside the home or doing a household task that requires greater physical energy. Male and female audiences are also targeted with distinctly different products. Diet pills and programs tend to be marketed to females, while males get the pitches for sports equipment.

Jacob, four years of age, sitting at the snack table said, "I only eat cereal that makes muscles." Jacob pulled up his shirtsleeve and showed Alex his muscle.

Alex rolled his shirtsleeve up and said, "I eat muscle cereal too." They both laughed.

I asked Jacob, "How do you know what cereal makes muscles?"

Jacob responded, "Just watch TV. It will tell you."

Television is not going away. The task for parents and guardians is to think through how best to edit its content for children and how to control its place in their lives. A few suggestions for preschoolers:

- Go to public libraries for videocassettes and DVDs to borrow. These are often advertising-free.

- Join your boy regularly for some of his television viewing. Discuss his opinions about what he is watching.

- Avoid using television viewing as a reward ("If you eat all your vegetables, you can watch television longer.").

- Play games with your children that reinforce activity rather than passive television viewing.

- Work out an overall balance between television and time for other activities.

TOYS AND GAMES REINFORCE IDEAS ABOUT GENDER DIFFERENCES

Starting at birth, boys receive different types of toys than girls. Such differences cannot be explained purely by the children's preferences. The beliefs of parents and other gift givers play a major role.

My own observation is that children display clear and early differences in their preferences for toys. Boys gravitate toward boisterous play. They like to manipulate objects and enjoy toys that make noises. Girls like much quieter activities and can concentrate for much longer periods of time. Girls often talk to their toys. Boys deconstruct them.

As I review current store catalogues, I still find that many promote toys based on assumptions about "boys' only" and "girls' only" play. Sections for girls and boys are separated. Girls' toys include dolls, dollhouse accessories, dollhouses, arts and crafts kits, toy beauty sets, and housekeeping toys. The boys' section offers sports-related toys, transportation toys, workbenches, and tools. This is also the only place that features Nintendo games and Darth Vader.

I am not suggesting that there is a conspiracy among manufacturers and advertisers to mass-produce messages that develop gender bias. Toy companies simply aim their products at the largest segment of population that uses them. As a by-product of that activity, these companies send messages about gender identity that children will internalize.

SAME-SEX PLAY MOLDS DIFFERENCES IN BEHAVIOR

In my preschool classroom, Carl was building with blocks. Other boys got involved in this activity with no need to ask for permission to join the play.

Jessica came by and started to put blocks on the building that the boys were assembling.

"This is only for boys!" Carl yelled.

"Yes this is only for boys!" said the other boys. Jessica simply walked away.

Some teachers might feel that they need to intervene to prevent such exclusion. However, I do not see this as exclusion. I see it as normal, same-gender play that often occurs among preschool children.

Boys will be boys—and girls will be girls—which is deeply influenced by the time they spend with same-sex peers. Preschool-age children often separate by gender, and this division leads to different sets of social skills, style, expectations, and preferences. If most of the girls like to wear dresses to school, for example, the other girls may want to do the same. If most of the boys play ball, the other boys may learn to do that.

Peers often establish standards of right and wrong, delivering verbal rewards and punishments early on. I have heard preschool boys tell other boys, who are playing with purses in the dress-up area, "You are a girl, because you have a purse." If the boy doesn't drop the purse immediately they might make fun of him and tell him that he looks like a girl.

Preference for same-gender play begins at around age two-and-a-half for girls and age three for boys and then often lasts until the early adolescent years. Girls tend to play nearer adults and often play house and other games that require more verbal interaction. Boys may gather on the playground in single-sex groups or only invite children who are the same sex to their block play. The boys seem more concerned with dominance. "Who's in charge?" they ask. "Who's the boss?" They like roughhousing, tumble play, acting like superheroes.

BOYS IN GROUPS WORK OUT CODES

Jason, age four, is clicking his tongue to the following beat: "Click, click, click, click, click" (pause).

Brian, who is the same age, sits across from him at the snack table. He responds with, "Click, click."

They both laugh hilariously.

Jason, the creator of this new code, proceeds to use it several times throughout the day. He initiates it during story time gathering, outdoor play, bathroom time, and, of course, in his favorite place—the nap room.

While engaged in same-gender play, boys create group dynamics such as this one that are distinctly different than those created by girls. Cory loves to snap his fingers to the beat of a rhythm he creates. Brent loves to whistle. And Brian loves to just simply say, "Knock, Knock, who's there?"

As we look at language development, we find many differences between how boys and girls communicate. For boys, codes are ways to develop language. Boys' communication patterns include the following:

- Facial gestures (favorite is the sticking out of the tongue)
- Voice tone (usually loud)
- Voice alone (sentences that are brief and relevant)

Notice that much of the boys' communication patterns are non-verbal. Girls' communication patterns are often verbal. This may in part explain why so many boys are labeled as delayed in language development and placed in speech and language classes.

Remember, however, that our current tools for assessing language measure verbal rather than non-verbal language. If we included all of the code making that goes on with boys, perhaps they would not appear to be as far behind as we think they are.

BOYS IN GROUPS FOCUS ON TASKS RATHER THAN PROCESS

Ryan came into the preschool classroom, took off his coat, hung it on his hook, and started going around asking other preschool boys, "Do you want to be part of my mean dog pack?" I watched this carefully. In response to this question, other boys either yelled, "*Yes*" or simply walked away without any reply. Those boys who said yes immediately got down on all fours and started to make loud growling sounds.

When Ryan thought he had enough "mean" dogs, he got down on all fours and began to make loud growling sounds too. The mean dog pack started to move around the room, growling and showing their "mean faces" at other children, especially the girls.

Many preschool boys play either by themselves or with one or two others without involving bigger groups. When play *does* take place in groups, verbal discussion seldom occurs. Instead, activity centers on visible action or the use of an object, such as gunplay, sword fighting, and string-and-bead helicopter games.

Boys who form groups and move into a group activity can quickly get in trouble. Often they don't think about what is going to happen when the "mean" dogs growl at children who don't want to be around this behavior. Many teachers feel the need to intervene and either redirect the dogs or change the behavior all together.

Something else that's quite subtle often happens in such situations. When gathered with peers of the same gender, boys tend to focus on performing tasks rather than negotiating a *process* for accomplishing tasks. When the task at hand is growling like dogs, boys will often launch into the activity without any discussion on how the dogs are to behave or function. At the preschool level, boys' forms of organization are loose. All it takes is a boy to yell out, "Let's build a space ship" and several of them will join in. Seldom do they pause to ask: How many blocks will it take? Who is the leader of the builders? How do we know if we have enough blocks? Is there enough room to build it?

Girls playing in groups tend to take more time organizing and planning. They manage the process by quickly determining how the group will function. When a girl makes a request to build a rocket ship, even at the preschool level, I usually observe a discussion of questions such as: How do we make it? Who is the leader? Is there enough room to make the rocket ship? Will everyone have a role? Compared to boys, girls show more sensitivity to the emotions of group members.

My observations of girls in groups often include:

- Girls congregate in "herds" or groups often.
- Girls engage in talking more frequently in the group.
- Girls greet newcomers with, "Hi, would you like to play with us?"
- Girls are primarily interested in children that they are playing with.

In contrast:

- Boys need larger spaces to play in groups.
- Boys often engage in rough and tumble play.
- Boys often avoid talking to newcomers.
- Boys usually engage in more bodily contact through pushing and shoving.
- Boys are primarily interested in the use of objects in their play.

Given such differences, I'm not surprised when teachers reported to me that boys often have a more difficult time mastering cooperative learning. My theory is that boys' brains are not wired for considering the emotions of their peers and playmates. The goal of group play for preschool boys is to perform tasks. Girls, however, do take feelings into account. Their goal is to perform tasks in an organized fashion and include all members of the group.

One day I watched a group of preschool girls playing grocery store in the drama play area. First, they organized the shelves with boxes and canned goods on separate shelves. Second, they discussed who was going to work the cash register. There was some disagreement because two girls wanted to be at the cash register at the same time. The group decided that the two girls would take turns. One would be the bagger and the other would run the cash register and then there would be a change in roles. The other girls' roles were to enter the grocery store and purchase items. Third, the girls had to decide what they were going to wear and started to select items of clothing that were hung in the dress-up area. Fourth, they needed something to carry the groceries in. They looked around and found some bags and suitcases. Fifth, the buying started to take place. All this organization took about 15 to 20 minutes.

In the meantime, one boy decided to rob the store. He ran towards the cash register and took the money out—a task that he completed in less than 30 seconds. "Teacher, he took our money!" yelled the girls.

A similar incident occurred when Josiah yelled out to David and Ralph, "Let's play hockey!" There was no hockey equipment around, but that didn't stop them. The boys simply improvised, taking plastic railroad tracks and a cup from the house area.

Josiah then grabbed a pillow from the book area and said, "This is the goalie." Then they began to hit the cup with the tracks.

David hit the cup into the pillow and Josiah yelled, "You made a goal!"

The three boys jumped up and down singing, "We made a goal, we made a goal!"

And that was their hockey game. There was no discussion of what roles the players were to perform. However, there was lots of vigorous hitting, jumping, and yelling.

Preschool teachers often allow the grocery store play but stop the hockey play. In reality, both types of play can be fun and healthy. Both kinds of activity need to be encouraged and allowed. Sure, boys' play will require a teacher who makes sure that the other children in the classroom watch out for the flying cup. But if we want to encourage social interactions, then we need to accept the different ways that boys and girls develop.

Vivian Paley reported that when girls played mothers and princesses they played with the same needs in mind as boys who played Darth Vader and Luke Skywalker—the need for power (Paley, 1984). When girls played mothers and princesses, they sometimes shake their fingers at the baby dolls or other girls and yell, "Don't you do that again or I might have to spank you!" This statement is one that gives girls power, much like boys who say "May the force be with you" and then start a swordfight. Remember, some princesses have practiced beheading!

A brief review

Chapter 1 suggests some significant differences between boys and girls and offers ideas for responding to them. Following are ideas that I often share with parents, guardians, and educators:

- **Remember that boys might demonstrate empathy differently than girls.** Early childhood professionals can benefit by helping boys to *demonstrate* their feelings rather than merely discussing them. (Look for related suggestions in Chapter 4 of this book.)

- **Allow for boys' brains to go into "pause state" after completing tasks.** Don't be surprised if boys take much longer than girls to complete an assignment, or even if they completely forget the assignment. Expect boys to compartmentalize the activity; they do best when focusing for long periods on one task and not as well when required to move rapidly from task to task.

- **Remember that boys have higher levels of testosterone, which stimulates action.** For them, movement is a requirement. This is another area where you may see differences between boys and girls. His brain is built for action, hers for talking; he does, she communicates. Without the chance to push, climb, run, or rock, boys are more likely to cause havoc in the classroom.

- **Allow for boys to develop language more slowly than girls.** Boys might have less word accumulation than girls and often use non-verbal language more frequently in their play.

- **Be prepared for boys to demonstrate more impulsive behaviors.** Your preschool boy may not be equipped to read social cues. Compared to girls, he might find it hard to gauge another person's emotional temperature or demonstrate empathy towards another person's pain. In classrooms, boys often act before they think. Teachers might say to a boy, "Remember when we talked about your hitting?" Chances are that he doesn't remember the discussion at all.

- **Keep in mind the important role that culture plays in child development.** Parenting styles and childrearing practices deeply influence the ways that boys and girls view themselves. Television and other media portray men as active and powerful and women as pretty and passive.

- **Look for nonverbal communication among boys.** Watch for boys as they hum and invent codes and chants.

- **Allow boys and girls to engage in different types of group play.** Boys commonly play in smaller groups with little forethought and lots of action. Girls often plan their experiences and carefully organize their group interactions. This difference may lead to conflicts and arguments.

Above all, we can all benefit by remembering not to confuse equality with sameness. This is a misunderstanding that does neither boys nor girls any good. Parents and educators can be so concerned with avoiding gender bias that they ignore visible differences between boys and girls. We can appreciate these differences while treating all children with respect. We do need to provide equal opportunities for boys and girls, but we must not expect the same behaviors. We can also use our new insights to recreate our educational environments.

After reflecting on my observations, I believe that boys are wired differently than girls. Early childhood professionals should act on the assumption that boys need opportunities to run more, climb higher and spin faster than girls.

Preschool practices must:

- Set up spaces for boys to run safely without someone saying, "Use your walking feet."

- Encourage and support boys with blocks to build structures that go "higher than their eyes."

- Encourage boys to spin indoors without someone saying, "Wait until you go outside."

If our practices do not match our beliefs then it is important for us to change. If you know that boys need to run everywhere, then the statement, "Running is for outdoors" conflicts with your belief and must be changed. We must evaluate our statements and make sure that our practices fit our belief.

Every day we can ask ourselves questions that might have the potential to transform our interactions with boys:

- How do my behaviors influence boys' and girls' understanding of themselves?

- Do I believe that there are "correct" ways of being boy or girl?

- Do I allow for differences between boys and girls?

- What messages do children receive from television and videos?

For educators, three questions are especially important:

- Based on current research and observation, what are my beliefs about boys?
- Do my practices, in my setting, reflect what I believe about boys?
- Do my beliefs and practices match? If not, how do I need to change?

The answers to these questions allow for exciting changes. As parents, teachers, and early childhood professionals, we can interact with boys in new ways. We can create a culture that allows boys to flourish as they grow into adulthood. We can establish "guardrails" for boys that offer stability, safety, and affirmation. We can take active steps to help boys become less of a bother and more of a joy in our daily lives. We can honor the differences between boys and girls and create avenues that support the growth of self-confident individuals.

Boys will not feel connected in an environment filled with messages that they don't belong. In continued chapters of this book specific steps you can take to create the kind of support that boys need is presented.

Below is a practice sheet to make sure your beliefs about boys fit your practices.
Fill in the empty spaces.

BELIEFS AND PRACTICES	
My Beliefs	*Practices that Support Beliefs*
1. Young children don't share often	1. Have multiples of toys
2. Boys like to run	2. Make space so they can run
3. Boys show anger physically	3. Provide boxes/pillows for hitting
4.	4.
5.	5.
6.	6.
7.	7.
8.	8.
9.	9.
10.	10.

2 Creating a "Boy-Friendly" Environment

The Environment

Sometimes to get a better look at what children saw in my classroom, I had to get down on my knees and take a look at what the environment invited them to do. Before children arrived on Monday, I asked: Do I have everything they need? What invitations are they going to receive? Asking these questions is a powerful way to start making sure that boys and girls feel welcome.

There are two common invitations that an environment can send:

- "Come on in—you can do it."
- "Come on in—let me do it."

The invitation that says "Come on in—*you* can do it" provides many play experiences that invite boys to take risks. Through appropriate risks, boys are encouraged to take chances, stick their necks out, climb higher, and cry when they are frightened. Taking these types of risks provides a firm emotional foundation for boys.

The invitation that says "Come on in—let *me* do it" prevents many experiences that are natural for boys. We issue this kind of invitation through common messages, such as:

"Look Out!"

"Don't Get Dirty!"

"Be Careful"

"Don't Run!"

"You'll be Sorry!"

Statements like these undermine boys' needs for independence and creativity. They prevent boys from growing up with hands-on knowledge of safety skills. You cannot learn to be safe by avoiding risks. Risks provide an avenue for practicing skills involved in making wise choices. Yet so many environments for boys lack provisions for them to explore, to create, to tear down, to build up, and to connect with the natural world.

INVITATIONS WE SEND	
Come on in and give it a try	*Come on in and let me do it for you*
• Accepts boys need to move often	• Encourages similarities
• Encourages risk taking	• Promotes compliance
• Supports creativity	• Enjoys products, not process
• Encourages being different	• Expects perfection

My experiences with young children lead me to believe that certain elements must be present every day for boys' robust growth. Caregivers have the task of creating an environment that invites boys to experience a rich natural environment—a place to mix mud, dig in sand, build dams, and live in caves.

What are those specific elements in an environment that send a welcoming invitation to boys? They include:

- Active play
- Moveable parts
- Running spaces
- Climbing spaces
- Water play spaces
- Digging spaces
- Roughhousing spaces
- Power spaces
- Solitary spaces

Following are some details about how you can create these environments for boys in your life.

ACTIVE PLAY

Active play is not a space *per se* but a habitat for learning. It can occur everywhere, throughout the day. Active play means that children are standing up more than sitting down. Many boys prefer to stand up when doing art, playing with clay and building. Chairs can be stacked in a corner; if boys want one, they can get it themselves. Remember, their brains tell them to "move, move, move as much as you can."

Active play allows boys to take objects from one area to another. Carlos filled a suitcase full of blocks, dishes, legos and books. He closed the suitcase and walked over towards the block area. Pointing to his suitcase, he yelled, "I'm going to work and I have everything I need in here."

Boys do not view play as activity that occurs in an isolated space, such as playing with blocks in the block area, dishes in the house area, or books in the library. They see play as an integrated experience. This does *not* mean that we eliminate centers in our preschools. It simply means that centers are the *starting* place and the *ending* place for lots of adventures that happen throughout the environment.

Active play happens in spaces that have different textures (carpet, tile, sand, cement, grass) and uneven spaces for climbing (tree stumps, boulders, ramps, bricks). This gives boys a chance to use large muscles, cross midline, and move in a way that challenges the brain and the body.

Active play also includes choices. For many boys, choices happen most often during play with art, small toys, blocks, and dress up. Structure these spaces and activities with the idea that boys often will:

- Move objects from one place to another.
- Need more space then girls.
- Create messes.
- Not make a plan for using the material they have.

Also remember that the amount of time a boy spends at an activity depends on his interest and the relevancy of the experience.

Eddie was standing on a tree stump and yelled, "I might need a little help here!" I went over and asked, "What kind of help do you need?"

"A hand that's ready to catch me if I fall," Eddie responded. Eddie thought he could handle this situation but wanted a hand nearby just in case.

Moveable parts

Someone at a workshop once asked me, "If you had only one thing that you could provide in an environment for boys, what would that be?"

Without hesitation my answer was, "Moveable parts." If play does not involve the boy's body through movement, then it will not involve his brain.

Learning takes place for a boy when he moves objects and makes changes. When he takes a broom and tries to sweep up dirt on a cement sidewalk, he learns the difference between heavy and light, fast and slow, and *some* and *all*. Brooms and rakes are wonderful moveable parts that many programs only provide for the caregiver or other staff members. A broom or a rake to a boy is not an object for cleaning up but a horse that gallops, a sword for a pirate, a dirt mover, and much more.

We can be harmful when we remove rather than reinforce children's opportunities to move—to run, roll, climb, jump, and attempt to fly. Boys like to fill tubs and baskets with all sorts of stuff and carry them to a "hidden

Moveable parts

MOVABLE PARTS

Here is a partial list of moveable parts that are free or inexpensive:
- Tires for rolling
- Plastic bins with wheels
- Mops
- Hand Carpet Sweepers
- Ropes
- Baskets with handles
- Blocks
- Old Garden Hoses
- Scooters
- Tire Pumps
- Plungers
- Nets
- Shopping Carts
- Buggies/strollers
- Frisbees
- Steering Wheels

place." They enjoy the opportunity to climb up a loft that can be turned into a pirate ship or a tree house. They want to run with a wagon filled with sand, hoping to miss other children on their way. Movement fuels the brain.

Charlie would take a chair in the classroom and run back and forth with it for twenty minutes a day. He often knocked down children as he ran—not because he wanted to hurt them but because he couldn't see them. The children who were being knocked over soon figured out what to do. When Charlie came a running with his chair they simply yelled, "He's coming" and then they ran out of his way.

Three boys in my preschool classroom found a wagon and started to fill it up with lots of different items from around the classroom. When they thought the wagon could take no more they started to move with it around the classroom.

Curious, I stopped them and asked, "What are you doing?"

"We are moving. We don't like this spot."

"Where are you moving to?" I asked.

"We don't know," they replied instantly, "but we will let you know when we get there."

It doesn't matter to them where they are going, I said to myself. *It only matters that they are able to move.*

RUNNING SPACES

If left to choose, most boys instinctively seek the joy of running. From a muscular-skeletal standpoint, the years between birth and the early twenties are key to building a solid foundation of muscles and joints that will operate properly for a lifetime. For young boys, this foundation is built only one way—through unstructured, spontaneous movement. Crawling, rolling, walking, throwing, and (most importantly) running are vital to full physical functioning.

Testosterone spikes in preschool-aged boys can occur often throughout the day. During these spikes the brain says to the body: *Run!* As teachers, we need to respond by providing more spaces for running, both outdoors and indoors.

You can design spaces that allow boys to do spontaneous running without crashing into tables or cabinets or disrupting other children's activities. For example, use tape to mark off expressways throughout the room.

Playing with capes and other superhero props also encourages boys to run.

Hallways are a great place to run as well. Where did we come up with the rule "No running in the hallway"? Let's change that to, "Make sure you run in the hallway!"

A mother brought her boy to my preschool classroom one morning when considering whether to enroll her son. She noticed that the boys were sometimes running from one area to another in the classroom. She frowned. Her son looked up and noticed the expression of disapproval.

"Mom, what's wrong?" the boy asked.

The mother responded, "The boys are running and I am worried they might get hurt."

The boy looked up at her, smiled, and replied, "Mom, you don't have to worry. They are good at running."

She enrolled her son that day.

If boys lose the right to run—the right to spontaneous, unstructured movement—then we increase the risk that they will develop a lack of confidence in their bodies along with obesity, heart disease, joint replacements, and a long list of other horrors.

CLIMBING SPACES

One of my fondest memories of childhood is about climbing to the top of a small hill in the field near our home and yelling, "I'm the king of the castle and you're the dirty rascal." The hill was not really that big, but I thought I was at the top of Mt. Everest.

Boys need the opportunity to feel bigger and higher, enjoying the feeling of power and amazement as they make it to the top.

Trees offer the most natural and spontaneous experience of climbing. If you are worried about children falling, then keep the tree trimmed to a height that will permit boys to reach the top. Remember that when boys climb trees they often yell out the Tarzan call to tame any nearby savage beasts.

No trees? Then provide a good and inexpensive prop for climbing, also known as a ladder. Adults often fear that children might fall, but my experience is that boys hang on as they climb up with much care and precision. If using tall ladders frightens you, then start out with stepladders. Give the boys practice being "taller then they are."

Climbing spaces

Climbing spaces

Here are some easy-to-find and inexpensive equipment that allows climbing:
- Oil barrels that can be buried in the ground at the base
- A mound of earth on the playground with grass planted on it
- Large ropes with knots, tied to the top of the swing bar
- Slides that children can climb up either way
- Tree forts
- Indoor lofts with ladders and nets for climbing
- Large boulders, tree stumps, and sand hills

I once asked a mountain climber, "Why do you do such a dangerous activity?"

He replied, "I have been climbing all my life. I worry more about being killed in a car accident on the way to a climb."

I thought about this response for a long time. When we provide climbing spaces for boys, they get to develop large muscles *and* skills for self-control. Boys learn how to climb high, and what they need to do to make it safely to the top.

WATER PLAY SPACES

Jacob, Carl and Sam were vigorously digging in the sand. Their hole was getting deeper and deeper. Carl got a hose and started to fill the hole with water.

Jacob and Sam, still digging, yelled, "Let's fill it up to the top with water and then we can go swimming."

As the water kept rising in the hole, the boys began to notice that the sides of the hole were caving in.

"Turn the hose off," yelled Jacob.

Carl ran over and turned it off.

The boys stood looking at the hole filled with water. Then they got down on their knees and started to pat the sand around the hole until it looked liked mud. The sides were still caving in, so the boys decided to remove the water with their shovels. They soon concluded that using shovels was slow and difficult.

At that point Sam started to make a gutter in the sand with his shovel and noticed the water was moving out of the hole. The other boys began the same process.

Jacob, Carl, and Sam worked for over twenty minutes on this activity. Access to water enabled them to discover something about engineering from a simple activity.

To a child, water seems like the breath of life. Water is the element that allows boys to pour, scoop, and dam. Water beckons a boy to keep exploring.

As I visit early childhood settings around the country, I often observe that water play is missing. When I ask teachers why they don't use water, they usually say, "Children get too wet." Yet children can easily dry off, clean up, and they usually have changes of clothing. Let's make water spaces available both indoors and outdoors.

Indoor water tables are usually too small, and children are expected to share them. Instead, use plastic wading pools on tables to create a larger space for more water. Provide cups, plastic bottles, scoops, caps, stones, and other objects that sink and float.

Water provides great opportunities not only for sensory experience but also for mathematical experience. As a child pours and measures, he learns about volume, weight, and amounts. As boys play together as engineers they learn to redirect water flow, stop flood damage and create new systems of drainage. Providing vinyl gutters, cut in various sizes, will extend this engineering. Adding sand or soil to the water really extends these possibilities.

Having access to an outdoor water source is extremely important. Using different kinds of hoses and pipes, you can create variety in water flow. In warmer climates, water makes puddles and small rivers. In colder climates, water freezes and you can add hand drills for drilling holes in the ice. Who knows what lurks underneath that ice—perhaps a large fish, waiting to be caught.

Water equipment includes:
- Large watering cans
- Water pumps
- Hoses
- Shovels
- Wood for making dams
- Plastic tubes
- Sand for making mud
- Shells, stones
- Spray bottles
- Turkey basters

Water play spaces

DIGGING SPACES

Jerry, age four, was digging in the sand area. He had a shovel and was carrying his sand over to a spot near the swings. The sand began to pile as he spent many minutes just digging, hauling, and dumping.

As I walked by, Jerry asked, "Do you think I can make this hill as tall as the swing set?"

I responded, "It is getting bigger with each shovel load of sand that you bring."

"Yeah," he responded. "I am making a sand hill so big that when I swing I will be able to kick it with my feet."

I was so glad that there was enough sand for him to believe he could build a big hill.

Do you remember making sand cakes when you were a child? There was no exact recipe for them, and they changed depending on the natural material available to you. Perhaps your sand cake's shape emerged from a bucket turned upside down, or from a large tin can that made imprints, or from a kitchen cake pan that made the best upside-down cake. To these delicious-looking cakes you added greens from dandelions, stones, small flowers, or sticks for candles.

So many children today are looking for the same kinds of sand experiences but can't find the sand. Sandboxes have been made smaller and smaller. Boys have a hard time finding spaces that allow them to "Dig to China."

Yet sand is one of the most natural ingredients for play. It moves with the wind, it sifts through holes of various sizes, and it allows you to create mud sculptures by adding water.

Sand permits boys to engage in a process that builds critical thinking and the ability

Digging Spaces

to solve problems. It encourages future architects, designers, plumbers, bridge makers, builders and, yes, even chefs.

Sand doesn't have to be only an outdoor experience. It can be put under tables, in the kitchen area, and of course in the block area.

My observation of boys' sand play is what prompted me to provide this beginning list of sand supplies:

- Shovels
- Buckets
- Scoops
- Plastic tubes
- Funnels
- Rocks
- Old pots and pans
- Bowls
- Spoons
- Sifters
- Film canisters
- Tubs
- Bones
- Shells

Shovels that you provide for digging need to be real and sturdy. Many hardware stores have shovels that fit a child, with round edges, and are heavy enough, but not too heavy, for children. They cost more than other shovels, but they last longer. This type of shovel permits that necessary digging that boys require towards their journey to "China."

ROUGHHOUSING SPACES

Dameon was a preschooler who would hit children throughout the day. He had an unmet need for "power." One day I watched Dameon go towards Carol with his fist in the air ready to hit her. I took a swimming noodle out of the box, and said to Dameon, "On Guard!"

Dameon smiled at me and grabbed another noodle and said, "On Guard!"

Laughing and giggling, we both started striking each other with the pretend swords. This play lasted about twenty minutes. Of course, other children joined in the fun, but they didn't stay as long as Dameon.

When Dameon's mom brought Dameon to school the next morning, she asked me, "What happened yesterday at school? Dameon said it was the best day he ever had." I knew from that moment that boys crave chances to fulfill their unmet need for power, and that we can help them meet that need in affirming, appropriate ways.

Roughhousing is a style of interaction for boys. It is an expression of life. Boys in particular have a real fascination with superhero play. It allows them to laugh and giggle in an exuberant release of physical energy.

While reviewing the literature on rough and tumble play over the last fifteen years, I have discovered no research indicating that roughhousing causes violence. This kind of social play is not always "nice." Even so, allowing for appropriate roughhousing gives boys the chance to negotiate power and experience how other children react. Roughhousing is more than playing—it is a way to explore the world.

When I got down on all fours in the preschool classroom, this was an open invitation for the children—usually boys—to jump and try to bring me down to the floor. They respond not with the desire to hurt but with a need to demonstrate strength. Rough and tumble play such as this is not an open invitation to world wide wrestling but a chance to pretend to kick and chop.

I am firm about what is roughhousing and what is hurting. When a child lifts his hand up to punch me, I say, "That has crossed the line into hurting. Grab my leg or arm instead. That is acceptable."

When we create trusting environments for roughhousing, self-expression is encouraged and the need for unhealthy competition is removed. Trust develops from roughhousing when:

- The danger of harm is removed.
- The environment creates safe opportunities for risk taking.
- The people who respond are predictable and reliable.
- Children are encouraged to develop "power" in appropriate ways.
- Adults listen and watch without judgments.
- Adults create opportunities for children to express feelings without being ridiculed.
- Children's thoughts and actions are viewed as significant.

To allow for roughhousing, rearrange equipment and materials so boys have the necessary room. Have mats available for safe landings. Provide capes, ropes, and nets for running and capturing.

POWER SPACES

Personal power is not based on dominance over others. It is an ability to make choices and produce results. A skill that is used *with* and *for* others. It is based on a sense of self worth.

If boys grow up without an appropriate sense of personal power, they may learn to act without regard for the other people around them. It is amazing what children and adults will do to achieve a sense of power, even if it means hurting or killing others. Consider that most of the high school killings in the last several years have been perpetrated by males. They came from families of various income levels. They came from different parts of the country and different races. I believe that they shared one thing in common—a lack of true personal power.

When we fail to provide boys in early childhood settings with safe opportunities to develop personal power, they may respond by creating conflicts and chaos: hitting other children, destroying materials, and, in general, making "all hell break loose."

After I walk into a setting for young children, I can tell within minutes whether opportunities for developing personal power exist. It is a feeling that smacks you in the face. I ask myself the following questions:

What choices do children have in this environment? Do they have the power to decide where, when, and whether activities take place? Some children come in with hesitation and take time to make choices. Others run as fast as they can to their favorite activity. We can create environments that are safe for both kinds of children.

Can children move objects from one play area to another? For example, can children bring blocks to the outdoors to bury them in the sand? Can they bring a wood airplane to the art area and paint it a different color?

I was in a preschool setting and children were putting dress-up clothes on in the house area. After they finished putting on the clothes, they started to walk towards the block area.

The teacher looked at them and said, "The dress-up clothes stay in the house area."

"We are going to work," the children said.

"Not in the dress-up clothes," she responded.

I went up to the teacher and whispered in her ears that she better get naked.

She looked at me, shocked.

"You came to work in your dress-up clothes from your house," I continued. "That is what the children were playing—going to work in their work clothes."

Do adults avoid questions and comments that are irrelevant or intrusive to children? An example is: "How many blocks did it take to build that structure?" We would not go up to professional builders and ask that question.

Are the rules so restrictive that they prevent children from developing problem-solving skills? Some restrictive rules are: "Go up the ladder and down the slide." "Only build as high as your eyes." "Sit on your chair and put your napkin in your lap before you eat."

I want to create an environment where children can use loud voices rather than "inside voices." For boys, talking softly is not normal.

Gerald grabbed a garden hose that was hanging on the wall and ran over to the house area. He raised the hose over his head and started to make a hissing sound, vigorously moving the hose from side to side. After he was finished he yelled, "You don't have to worry about the school burning down. I put out the fire and saved the school!" You could tell from his voice and his stance that he felt personal power.

SOLITARY SPACES

As a young child, I made caves inside and outside. All I needed to make a tent alongside a wire fence were some blankets and stones for counterweights. Then I would crawl inside and make the outside world disappear.

Boys need places that provide solitude. Solitary spaces are not time-out chairs or punishment places. They are chances to rest the brain and body. Preschool teachers do a much better job of developing spaces for *groups* of children than finding spaces for children to be by themselves. Boys need a "cave" that they can enter to "zone out."

Offer blankets and sheets for boys to throw over tables and chairs. You can also help children make caves by providing:

- Large boxes and pillows
- Sheer curtains for throwing over clotheslines or rope
- Barrels with a large crawl hole
- A cupboard with the door removed and a pillow placed inside
- Cushions placed under tables
- Saw horses or tables with blankets to throw over them

Gerald, age four, went over to a stack of blankets and piled as many as he could into his arms. He walked over to a table and started to put the blankets underneath. Then he took one blanket and threw it over the top of the table. Next, using a roll of masking tape from the art area, he taped the blanket to the table. When he finished, he crawled under the table and laid down on the blankets he placed there.

Craig saw all this. He went over to the blanket-covered table and asked Gerald, "Can I come in?"

"No," Gerald said. "It is my resting place."

Boys are often looking for a "cave" for resting. Let's make sure we provide the materials necessary to design and build them.

"A playful encounter with the world does not supply the right or wrong answers to problems but it expands the avenue for finding solutions," write Bev Bos and Jenny Chapman in *Tumbling Over the Edge: A Rant for Children's Play*. "Players can looks outside the box or known body of knowledge to find possible solutions to the myriad problems, which haunt and challenge every generation of people who inhabit his fragile and fascinating space called the planet Earth" (Boss and Chapman, 2006).

The spaces for boys that I present in this chapter are all designed to promote the playful encounters that Bos and Chapman describe. Our purpose, as always, is to provide a rich and friendly environment for children, including boys. We can recreate our environment to help boys' brains make new connections. We can create spaces that welcome their boundless physical energy. We can create a boy friendly culture that sustains them throughout their entire lives.

3 The Curriculum

Recently I visited a preschool classroom that was involved in a cooking activity. The teacher brought a few children at a time to a table with the necessary ingredients and talked about how to make biscuits.

When it was time for Sam, Jerry, and Kevin to take their turn, the teacher explained that she had something very exciting for them to do. She told each one of them to sit on a chair and explained that they were going to make biscuits, and that they could then put jam on the biscuits for lunchtime.

"Do you like biscuits?" the teacher asked.

"I don't know," Jerry said. "What are they?"

"Are they like the kind that KFC has?" Sam asked.

Kevin said, "I don't like them."

The teacher continued, showing them how they would need to combine flour and water to make the dough.

Kevin again said, "I don't like biscuits."

"You will like this biscuit because you are going to make it," the teacher said.

Sam began by adding flour into a bowl. He almost emptied the whole bag into the bowl.

Jerry added a lot of water and Kevin began to stir with a large spoon. It didn't work for him, so he put his hands into the mixture and began to squeeze.

That looked like fun to Sam and Jerry. They also put their hands inside the bowl and began to squeeze. So now we had Sam, Jerry and Kevin squeezing flour and water together while chanting: "Squeeze, Squeeze, Squeeze, and Squeeze."

The teacher responded by saying, "Take your hands out and go over and wash them." The boys went over to the sink and began to rinse off the flour and water. They noticed large pieces that were not going down the drain. They tried to make smaller pieces by squeezing again. The teacher went over to the sink, and reminded them that they were supposed to be washing their hands.

Finally the boys finished washing. The teacher called them over and showed them the biscuits that she had made for them. "You can go play now," she said.

As he walked away, Kevin said, "I don't like biscuits."

Let children drive the curriculum

This is an example of curriculum that came from outside (the teacher) rather than inside (the boys). When the boys started squeezing and chanting, their learning came from the inside. The activity was exciting. When the teacher stopped the activity and changed it to hand washing, the boys' learning stopped.

As this example indicates, we sometimes focus on issues that are not relevant or real for boys: Will it look like a biscuit? Will they have a biscuit for lunch? Are they learning how to make a biscuit? These issues are based on curriculum ideas that come from an external source—the teacher. In reality, boys need a chance to reach inside their "gut" and pull out ideas that are important at their stage of development.

During my 32 years of working with children and their families in early childhood settings, my practices have changed. As a beginning teacher, I carefully planned my curriculum in advance, often relating it to an overriding theme or concept. Today, as a seasoned teacher, I advocate that children have enough materials to create based on their own ideas and internal drives.

Children should drive the curriculum. Our job is to find ways to support their learning and allow the curriculum to emerge. For children, curriculum is always about the process. We never should *model* or direct an activity while they are creating. The hardest part for teachers is to just stand back and watch the unfolding of learning.

Allow for choice and change

Boys need a curriculum that supports their interest in changing activities—one that creates a climate of suspense, surprise, and excitement. Change forces boys to rethink programs and patterns. In so doing, the possibility for new learning emerges.

Allowing children to introduce change supports higher levels of learning. This is the kind of learning that physically "rewires" sections of the brain.

Children must have the chance to repeat tasks, decide when they are completed with an activity, and then choose a new activity. Boys are especially interested in their quest to use lots of materials in different ways. I have learned to trust children and appreciate their many learning styles.

This chapter suggests activities within a preschool setting that can help boys develop a healthy self-concept and balanced ideas of gender.

Many of these activities were attained at a conference titled Good Stuff for Kids, held each year by Bev Bos and Michael Leeman (www.turnthepagepress.com).

Art comes from the inside

Many people put crafts and art together in the same category. They are not the same. Crafts are often directed by the adult, with product as the goal. Art is directed by the child, with process as the goal. In order for art to be appreciated by boys they must be free to experiment with larger-than-life materials.

Most boys do art experiences in a solitary fashion with perhaps no real goal at the beginning. Every effort a boy makes needs to be viewed as unique and peculiar to his own style and energy, as an artist. Art never has to be anything. Art is not to take home but to enjoy the process of doing.

When boys do art, they usually need to stand up, use bigger brushes, become as active as possible. Paper must be at least as long as a boys arm spread. Boys need easels that are full body length so they can stand up and move art utensils using their whole body. When I watch boys paint at the easel they prance around while painting the paper, their hands, arms and sometimes their bodies.

Following is a list, including art tools and materials, that should be made available on a regular basis.

Rubber Band Swatters

Materials:
- Large rubber bands
- Wood dowels of different sizes
- Tape

Explore by:
- Taking large rubber bands and cutting them in strips. Attach to a dowel using heavy-duty tape.
- Dipping the swatters in paint and slapping against large sheets of paper taped to the wall.
- Being careful not to intrude with the words "not so hard."

Bombs Away

Materials:
- Nylons
- Sand
- Paint
- Paper
- Ladder

Explore by:
- Taking nylons (knee-highs) and filling with sand (usually one to two cups).
- Tying a knot in the nylon, trapping the sand in the toe.
- Having a ladder with a ledge.
- Putting some paint in plastic bowls on the ladders ledge.
- Climbing the ladder, dipping the nylons with sand in the bowls of paint and yelling, "Bombs Away!" as they

Bombs Away

and placing the brushes by some paint. Watch what the boys do with them.

Boys have more difficulty using small finger tools. This provides them the opportunity to use their fists. Remember: most boys would rather stand up to paint at a table.

Back Massage Brushes

Materials:

- Different kinds of massage tools
- Paper
- Paint

Explore by:

- Going to your discount stores or outlet stores that sell massage tools. There are many that are used for your back that make great paint tools. I use one that has four bumpy, rubbery balls with a handle. It looks like a large wheeled car.
- Placing the massage brushes by some paint with large sheets of paper and watch what happens.
- Encouraging big movements with this activity. This is great for cross the midline experiences.

drop the paint-loaded nylons onto the paper-covered floor.

- Being aware—this is lots of fun.

Horse Brush Painting

Materials:

- Horse Brushes
- Paint
- Paper

Explore by:

- Going to a Pet Store or Farm Grainary and purchasing brushes that are used on horses. They are soft and rubbery.
- Having large sheets of paper at a table

Bottle Brushes and More

Materials:
- Different sized bottle brushes
- Paper
- Paint

Explore by:
- Going to a hardware or kitchen utensil store and looking for large handle art tools. Examples are bottle brushes, toilet bowl brushes, etc. Many boys do not like small brushes—the bigger the better.
- Putting these tools by the easel with large sheets of paper.

Shaving Cream Raking

Materials:
- Cans of Shaving Cream (one per child)
- Plastic Rakes
- Smooth Surfaces

Explore by:
- Giving a child a can of shaving cream and letting him spray it on a table surface. Remember: they need lots of shaving cream.
- Providing small plastic rakes that you can get at garden shops. Watch the experimentation that takes place with this one. Many boys will take the rake and pull it through the shaving cream leaving tracks. Soon, they might discard the rakes and paint with their hands, arms and other body parts.

Ping Pong Ball Art

Materials:
- Ping Pong Balls
- Boxes with lids
- Paper
- Paint

Explore by:
- Going to discount stores and buying packages of ping pong balls.
- Finding a box with a lid, e.g. large shoeboxes. Putting a piece of paper in the bottom of the box.
- Dipping the ping-pong balls into paint and dropping them into the box.
- Putting the lid on and letting the boys shake the box as hard as they can. When they finish, take the lid off the box, take the paper out and see what happened.
- Using golf balls and marbles can expand this.

Broom Painting

Materials:

- Large sheets of paper
- Paint
- Brooms with long handles
- Squeezable Containers

Explore by:

- Putting paper on the floor.
- Putting different colors of paint into squeezable containers.
- Having boys squeeze paint on paper.
- Giving them brooms with long handles for sweeping through the paint.
- Having soapy water close by for cleaning off brooms and feet.

Toilet Plungers (this is my favorite art tool for boys)

Materials:

- Toilet Plungers
- Sponge
- Paper
- Paint

Explore by:

- Going to a hardware or discount store and purchasing a toilet plunger, making sure to get one with the tall handle.
- Rolling out a large sheet of paper on the floor.
- Having a sponge with paint on it in a pan.
- Dipping the plunger onto the sponge and plunging the paper with it. It takes

Toilet Plungers

them a long time to get the plunger off the paper because of the suction. That's the great part of this activity. This provides such *power*.

- Having soapy water close by for washing off plungers

More ideas

Just walk through a hardware or kitchen supply center and look at what might be used for art tools. Yard and garage sales provide another, often cheaper, source. This is a small sampling:

- Good quality paper
- Spray bottles
- Scrapers
- Dog toys
- Clay rather than play dough (available through art catalog or art supply stores)
- Straws
- Large paintbrushes
- Large paint rollers

- Mops
- Brooms
- Different kinds of shoes for print
- Tape

Many boys do not go to the art area as often as girls because of the lack of large movement tools. Their lack of fine motor control prevents them from using small brushes at the easel. Their lack of spatial boundaries prevents them from using small sheets of paper. Their need to move prevents them from standing at an easel that is to small or sitting in a chair to do art. Our responsibility is to provide an extensive variety of tools and materials so that boys can experiment and become comfortable expressing themselves.

Cassius at the art area with a toilet bowl plunger says, "I could do this plunging all day." His art not only provides him with artistic expression but a chance for him to explore his power.

SCIENCE FOR BOYS

Traditionally science was the one area that boys excelled in. As the educational system started to remove the opportunity for exploring, playing and digging in the elements, boys' interest and scores started to plunge. Science is everywhere, all around us, not an area. When boys learn science they are engaged in a process that builds critical-thinking skills and the ability to use new information in the problem-solving process. The best way for boys to learn science is to participate in it and observe the results. Boys want to be engaged in the world.

Cory came up to me in the classroom and said, "Dan, I know how to make it night time."

"How?" I asked.

"Close your eyes and it will be night."

"Open your eyes and it is daytime," explained Cory.

"Try it," demanded Cory.

I closed my eyes and said, "It is dark."

"Now open them," said Cory.

I opened my eyes and said, "It is light now."

"See I told you," responded Cory.

Yes, I could have explained to Cory the true facts about opening and closing your eyes and what makes the earth turn to night and day. What Cory really needed was to explain to me what he discovered about opening and closing his eyes. That is true *science*.

Following are a few simple science ideas that can be used to expand knowledge and create questions.

Flower Pots and Pool

Materials:

- Clay Flowerpots (various sizes)
- Clear Plastic Bottles (various sizes)
- Plastic Wading Pool
- Dry Ice
- Gloves
- Dish Soap

Explore by:

- Cutting plastic bottles in half, lots of them. They can be used for measuring, pouring, mixing and digging.
- Using a small wading pool with water.
- Adding clay pots that the children can stack or pile on top of each other.
- Adding dry ice under the flowerpots and watching what happens. Most teachers are afraid of dry ice. Just don't let the children handle it and use gloves to place it under the flowerpot in the water.
- Adding liquid soap, etc. to see how the water changes.

Knox Gelatin Molds

Materials:

- Knox Gelatin
- Water
- Containers (various sizes)
- Pipets
- Food Coloring

Explore by:

- Buying packages of Knox gelatin
- Sprinkling gelatin on water to soften. Mixing ingredients and heating until dissolved.
- Pouring into containers of different sizes. Chilling until firm.
- Pushing pipettes down into the gelatin to release food coloring.
- Poking and manipulating the gelatin molds will end up in small pieces.
- Reheating the broken pieces will re-mold them.

Ice and Snow Sculptures

Materials:
- Clear containers (various sizes)
- Table salt
- Food coloring
- Pipets
- Water

Explore by:
- Freezing ice in many different containers.
- Using the big blocks of ice as a base, attach the other ice shapes to the big blocks. This can be accomplished with the use of table salt.
- Dripping food coloring on the sculpture if they want for color (where available, snow can be used in similar, creative ways).

Magnets

Materials:
- Magnets (various sizes)
- Paper clips
- Keys
- Buckles
- Metal cars

Explore by:
- Finding all kinds of magnets at the hardware store.
- Placing them on a table with items that the magnets will be attracted to e.g. large paper clips, metal cars, keys, belt buckles, etc. Stand back and watch the boys....

Playing with Air

Materials:
- Large garbage bags
- Straws
- Feathers
- Fans
- Hair dryers
- Black felt
- Paper plates

Explore by:

This activity can be done indoors and outdoors.
- Gathering materials that boys can use to "catch" air with.
- Running with large garbage bags, closing the bag when you think you have enough air and seeing if they will stay filled.
- Blowing air around with straws, trying to roll cotton balls, ping pong balls, cloth, etc.
- Putting feathers on a fan surface that has a screen and turning on the fan. Seeing how high the feathers will float in the air.
- Putting ping pong balls on a hair dryer spout. Turning on the hair dryer and seeing if the ping pong balls will float.
- Putting black felt on a paper plate and sticking it in the freezer. On those days when there are big snowflakes, taking the plate with black felt on it outside. Children will be amazed on how each snowflake is a different design and a different size.

Clean Mud

Materials:

- Bars of Ivory Soap
- Warm Water
- Rolls of toilet paper (white)
- Cheese Grater

Explore by:

- Using a cheese grater, let children grate soap (ivory soap bars) into a large plastic pan.
- Adding warm water. Stir soap to help it dissolve.
- Tearing toilet paper (the cheap kind) and adding it to water/soap solution. There is no amount for this recipe. Just keep adding the ingredients until the mixture feels right for you.
- Squeezing and feeling the clean mud. Don't expect the boys to make sculptures.

Bubble Makers

Materials:

- Dish Soap
- Large Bucket
- Glycerin
- Items to make bubbles

Explore by:

- Adding dish soap (less oil type) to water in a large bucket. Some people add glycerin, but it only needs to be used if you want the bubbles to last longer.
- Gathering as many tools as you possibly can imagine to use as bubble makers:
    - Baseball Hat Dryers
    - Plastic Pop Holders
    - Plastic Fly Swatters
    - Plastic large spoons with holes in them
    - Straws
    - Funnels
    - Slinkys
    - Plastic Strawberry Baskets

Take Apart and Put Together

One of a boy's greatest passions is wondering how things work. Boys love to take things apart and try to put them back together to figure out how they work. Some boys might just be interested in taking the same thing apart, over and over again. Others might be interested in taking something apart and adding things to it. All of this taking apart and putting together supports the mathematical and spatial intelligences. With this activity it is best to remember that "real things" are the best treasures.

Supplies:
- Small motors
- Toasters
- Mixers
- Old typewriters
- Small televisions
- Old radios
- Cameras
- Telephones

(Remember to remove all sharp parts and electric cords)

To help boys take things apart and try to put them back together, teachers will need to have available:
- Hammers
- Rubber mallets
- Screwdrivers
- Pliers
- Screws
- Tape
- Measuring tapes
- Goggles

Have heavy-duty bags available to take the parts home if they want to.

Hammers

Movement activities

If I like to move, does that make me "bad"? As I visit classrooms across the country I wonder if more and more boys aren't asking this question. In my experiences boys who aren't active are often labeled ADHD, placed in time-out chairs, separated from the rest of the group, or otherwise "in trouble."

There are many studies that document the overall benefits of movement and exercise, but the benefits for the brain are clear and simple. Preschool boys can have many spikes of testosterone during the day. This causes them to move around a lot, prance frequently, sit on the edge of their seats, tilt their chairs back and forth and sometimes knock over children who are in their way.

These forms of movement are not to be punished or discouraged but to be celebrated.

Joseph, who attended our school for two years, went on to kindergarten. His mother brought him over to the preschool one day to visit. When he came through the door, I noticed his face didn't look as full of life as it usually did.

I went over to him and said, "I am so glad to see you. We missed you. Are you having fun at your new big school?"

He looked at me and said, "We don't get to run at my new school and my shoes are always telling me to run."

I asked him, "Do your shoes want you to run now?"

Joseph replied, "Yes."

"Well, don't keep them waiting, start running," I replied.

Joseph took off running with a smile on his face.

My heart said to my brain, "I hope he continues to find a place that listens to his shoes."

If given the choice, boys would rather be outside then inside. It is crucial that we provide lots of opportunity for outdoor experiences that support their need to move, push, shove, climb and of course run.

To create opportunities for successful movement activities teachers need to:

- Keep the activity simple.
- Use activities that allow use of both sides of the body.
- Avoid directions that indicate left and right.
- Allow children not to participate.
- Rotate high energy experiences with low energy experiences.
- Begin with warm up and end with winding down.
- Create activities that are open-ended.
- Include adults moving with the boys.

Don't forget to bring back the many games you played as a young child. Boys today still want to play them:

- Motorboat, Motorboat
- Ring Around the Rosie
- London Bridge
- Red Rover, Red Rover
- Red Light, Green Light
- Simon Says
- Kick the Can
- Freeze Tag

The following is a sampling of additional creative movement activities for boys.

Sleeping Bag Dance

Provide a sleeping bag for each boy. Have them get inside and pretend to move in various ways with music. Suggest movements like pretending there are lots of spiders in the sleeping bag; pretending you are cold; pretending that you are really hot, etc.

Tug of War

Tie a rope around your waist and lay the rest of the rope in a line on the floor. Yell, "Tug of war." Watch how many boys come over and try to pull you.

Back-to-Back Rides

Have one child get on the floor on all fours. Make sure his back is flat. Have another boy lay his back flat against the other boy's back. That means his face will be looking at the ceiling and feet on the floor (crab-walk position). Ask the boy, facing the floor on all fours, to start moving. Be ready for lots of laughing and giggling as they try to move together.

Towel Dancing

Provide large bath towels for each child. Have the children pretend to get out of the bathtub and dry themselves to music. As they develop this skill you can have two boys place the towel around their backs and have each boy take each other's towel ends. They can move to music as they pull each other's towel.

Bag Movements

Take large pillowcases and see how many boys can get inside one. Have them try and move together.

Newspaper toss

Roll lots of old newspapers into balls. Place the newspaper balls inside a plastic bag. When you have one of those days when the boys seem to need opportunities for throwing, just simply take one of the paper balls out of the bag and throw it. Yell, "Snowball fight!"

Stretch Bands

Make stretch bands from three-foot lengths of wide elastic. Provide each child with a stretch band and try the following. Stand on one foot and use both hands to stretch it over your head. Hold the band in front of you and stretch it across your chest. Put the band behind you. Stretch using both hands. Create your own stretches.

Pretzel Pass

Provide each child with a straw, chopstick or dowel rod. Put a large pretzel on every other stick. Invite the children to pass the pretzels from one stick to another (remember: part of the fun of this activity is eating the pretzels).

Parachute Fun

Get a parachute from a surplus store or catalog. Lots of games and activities can be robust for boys:

- Have the boys run under the parachute after they raise it as high as they can.

- Have the boys run across the parachute, while the adults make waves with the parachute.

- Lift the parachute way up in the air and have all the children bring it behind their backs and sit on it (they will all be inside an igloo).

- Play foot monster. Have all the children sit down on the floor or ground with their legs out straight, under the parachute. The children need to pull the parachute tight under their chin. Have one of the children or adults get under the parachute and be the foot monster. The foot monster grabs a foot of a child and they scream and become a foot monster too. This goes on until everyone is a foot monster.

- Play cloud dancing. Play music and have the children pretend the parachute is a cloud. They prance around on top, very carefully, because they don't want to fall through the cloud.

Outdoor Play

I am so concerned with "static playgrounds" and the traditional uses that do little to stimulate boys' development. Playgrounds really fall short of providing movement that is essential to a child's development. Boys are usually not able to change the equipment to challenge themselves. The playground is a natural choice for many facets of learning. Boys can perform pushing swings, pulling wagons, lifting and carrying movable objects.

Here is some playground equipment that will support boys' development:

- Rope ladders
- Firefighter pole
- Large hoops
- Steering wheels
- Barrels and kegs
- Watering cans
- Tin pots and pans
- Horse saddles
- Rowboats
- Wheelbarrows
- Bicycle pumps
- Lumber
- Pulleys

MOVEMENT EXPERIENCES

Creating movement experiences for boys celebrates their need to be active by:

- Letting them move around a lot
- Letting them stand up rather than sit down
- Allowing them to act out stories
- Providing experiences for pushing, shoving, crawling, climbing, and running

The following are a few essential areas necessary on a playground that supports the development of boys.

Climbing

Few experiences provide more power for a boy then sitting at the top of a structure. Whether your climbing equipment consists of a ladder, jungle gym, monkey bars or a cargo net, you can help boys use their body in new and exciting ways.

Climbing

Balancing

Whether you use purchased balance beams or you make them yourself, there are endless possibilities for travel along the beam including: forward, backwards and sideward, on one foot, in slow motion and as quickly as possible. Balance beams allow boys to become the "tight rope walkers" that they have always dreamt about.

Tunnels

Most boys love tunnels. Tunnels are especially suitable for exploring the concepts of outside and inside, but can also be used for experiencing over, through, around, and under. Examples of tunnels can be plastic culverts, large cardboard boxes, rows of upright tires and wooden crates. Boys can imagine themselves finding treasures (left from pirates), hiding from someone, becoming cave dwellers, and much more.

Tunnels

Platforms

For boys, just being above ground can add an extra challenge. Boys who have platforms are often seen pretending to play dancers, actors, performing seals, magicians and of course King Kong. Platforms can be made from upright telephone cable spools, sturdy tables, solid wooden crates and large tree stumps.

Sand

First and foremost, sand with digging and pouring tools is a natural for constructive play for boys. Make sure you have enough to DIG TO CHINA. Check with pool companies that have sand mixtures that cats do not like. How often do boys practice careers like bakers (mixing their favorite recipes), scientists working on experiments, builders of dams, tunnel makers, etc.

Riding Toys

Maneuvering a riding toy along a pathway and around corners and obstacles does much to develop visual-motor skills and laterality for boys. Make sure the riding equipment is durable and that some equipment invites more than one rider. For example, bikes that have hitches for adding wagons, wagons that seat more then one child, shopping carts for filling and scooters for balancing are also essential for boys.

Slides

Remember that slides for boys are used to climb up rather than going down. It can be a chute for sending all kinds of items down. Perhaps a water slide. Boys benefit from using the slide in many different ways. As I watch boys, they go down the slide backwards, lying on their stomachs, flat as possible, with one leg bent and the other straight, or perhaps both legs bent.

I remember as a child, forming trains. Gathering as many children as I possibly could as they spread their legs around my waist and held on until the chain of children got so heavy we had nothing else to do but slide together.

Swings

Swinging is the closest thing to flying many boys will ever get.

Learning to pump to gain momentum, boys develop a sense of the midline of the body. Bring back the tire swing…it provides for lots of twisting, side by side, and other movements you can't get from manufactured swing sets. Boys will need to swing on their stomachs, stand up, and perhaps include more then one child. Boys' brains tell them to take risks. It is important that teachers make the surface under the swings safe for impacts.

Chapter Three: The Curriculum 55

Swings

Music experiences

Many boys have a hard time singing in tune because they often don't hear the tune. They hear the volume and pitch. Often they only remember the words that are relevant to them and can be acted out or shouted. Their favorite songs, finger plays and chants are those that are loud and require some form of movement.

Ranging from Mother Goose rhymes to Jump Rope chants to Folk singing to Contemporary vocals, music provides a bridge between oral communication and the written word.

Beyond helping to develop listening and speaking skills, stimulating imagination and assisting in memory development, music is just plain fun. Spontaneous singing comes from the cognitive and emotional sides of the brain.

Sometimes the best music of all is the boys' own creations. Many spontaneous songs are funny, silly songs repeated over and over again. Brian sat on a bike outside singing loudly, "My mom burnt pancakes, but I ate them anyway," over and over.

Songs, finger plays, and chants were never really written for group time. Boys need to sing everywhere all the time. Teachers need to reach inside themselves and pull out songs from their childhood and sing them. When our parents sang songs to us, they usually didn't gather the neighborhood children first.

Here is a collection of songs, finger plays and chants that boys seem to love. Remember when you sing make sure you are not afraid to be loud, boisterous and passionate about what you are singing.

Pirate Song

When I was one, I had some fun
On the day I went to sea.
I jumped aboard a pirate ship, (jump high, putting hand over one eye and making a sound like a pirate)
And the captain said to me.
"Oh, you go this way, that way,
(move side to side, don't forget to bump)
Forward, backward over the deep blue sea.
(Repeat to ten; make up responses as you go. I include movements of swordfighting, pretend spitting, etc.)

Benji Met the Bear

Benji met the bear
(put hand down to one side and show how small Benji is)
The bear met Benji
(Put hands up in the air and growl loudly)
The bear was bulgy
(make a round shape with hands over belly)
The bulge was Benji
(rub stomach like you just finished a good meal)

Chocolate Candy and Jelly Beans

Chocolate Candy and Jelly Beans
Put them in my pocket and put them in my jeans
Momma washed the clothes and this is what she said
AHHHHHHHHHHHHHHHHHHH
(hands over head, scream)
Chocolate Candy and Jelly Beans
All over the washing machine.

(Have children hang onto hands of as many children as they want and pretend to be a washing machine)

The Stars at Night

The stars at night go Twinkle, linkle link
Away up in the sky.
The moon at night goes, Blinka, blinka blink
It shines right in my eyes.
The skunk at night goes, stinka, stinka stink
I wished that he'd go by.
Oh, twinkle, linkle link
Oh blinka, blinka, blink
Oh, stinka, stinka, stink
Oh my!

(Have children hold noses for skunk and try to swish it away)

Chris Is His Name

Chris is his name
And pushing is his game.
You can catch him pushing,
In the sun and rain.
He is pushing high
He is pushing low
He is pushing, pushing, wherever he goes.
So if you want some pushing
And you don't know what to do
Just go ask Chris and he'll help you.

(Have children put their palm of their hand on someone's shoulder. They push when the word push is said)

Whooping Cough

Way down yonder a little way
A jaybird died from the whooping cough
He whooped so hard with the whooping cough,
He whooped his head and tail right off.

There's A Big Ship Sailing

There's a big ship sailing on the illy ally oh,
Illy ally oh, illy ally oh.
There's a big ship sailing on the illy ally oh,
Hey ho, illy ally oh.

(Don't forget to scream out the illy, ally oh)

If You Want to Catch a Fish

If you want to catch a fish, find a worm
If you want to catch a fish, find a worm
If you want to catch a fish,
Then you have to find a worm
If you want to catch a fish, find a worm.

(Don't forget to get on all fours on the floor looking for worms, when that line is sung)

Boom, Boom, Ain't it Great to Be Crazy!

A horse and a flea and three blind mice,
Sat on a curbstone shooting dice.
The horse he slipped and fell on his knee,
"Whoops," said the flea, "There's a
    horse on me!"

Chorus:
Boom, boom, ain't it great to be crazy!
Boom, boom, ain't it great to be crazy!
Giddy and foolish, the whole day through,
Boom, Boom, ain't it great to be crazy!
Way down south where bananas grow,
A flea steps on an elephant's toe.
The elephant cried with tears in his eyes,
"Why don't you pick on someone our size!"
(Chorus)
Way up north where there's ice and snow,
There lived a penguin and his name was Joe.
He got so tired of black and white,
He wore pink slacks to the dance last night.
(Chorus)

RHYMES, CHANTS AND FINGER PLAYS

Pat Wolfe states that, "Rhymes, Chants and Finger plays increase cognitive growth and supports memory development." I remember, still today, what the process is for a bill getting through Congress from the chant, *I'm Just A Bill* that was repeated on Schoolhouse Rock. This was a television program that aired every day after school. I know I was exposed to the process in Civics or American Government classes, but it was the chant that placed the process in my long-term memory.

Boys like riddles, jokes, chants and finger plays that often border on ridiculous. It stimulates laughter and creates connections to both sides of the brain. Boys make them up which supports language growth. Here are some examples:

Fatty Fatty

Fatty, fatty two by four
Can't get through the kitchen door.

Kindergarten Baby

Kindergarten baby,
Wash your face in gravy.

Happy Birthday to You

Happy Birthday to you
You belong in a zoo
You look like a monkey
And you act like one too.

Underpants

I see London,
I see France,
I see _____ underpants!

You can't sing these songs, finger plays and chants using an "inside voice." They have to be loud and inspire movement. My fear is that boys will stop singing eventually unless we bring back the "spirit" of the song. Music has so much power to it when we allow stomping, clapping and pushing. Remember, boys don't care if you sing off key or dance ungracefully. They do care if you don't sing and dance.

Music Using CDs

When using CDs with young children it is important to note that the artist doesn't know the children in your classroom. So the music might be too slow or too fast for the children you are working with. I generally buy CDs and play them to myself until I have memorized the songs and then sing the songs with children. That way I can tell if the children are ready to move to the next verse or if we need to sing it again. Boys often need to practice the song many times to place it in their memory. The following is a small sampling of CDs that seem to work with boys:

Still Growing, Tom Hunter

We've Been Waiting for You, Bev Bos, Michael Leeman, Tom Hunter

I Have a Box, Bev Bos, Michael Leeman, and Tom Hunter

Come on Over, Tom Hunter, Michael Leeman, Bev Bos

Singable Songs: Great With a Peanut Butter Sandwich, Raffi

American Folk Songs for Children, Peggy Seeger & Mike Seeger

Leadbelly Songs for Children, Leadbelly

Le Hoogie Boogie Louisana French Music for Children, Michael Doucet

Songs Children Love to Sing, Ella Jenkins

Fandegumbo, Julie Austin

Music from your body

Boys love to make music with their bodies and it can be a great introduction to rhythm. Talk to boys about what sounds a cough, burp, sneeze, yawn, hiccup, giggle and snore make. Then ask them to show you how each sound makes their body move. Have boys explore how many sounds they can create with different body parts (hands, feet, tongue, and teeth). You will be amazed how many body parts boys can come up with.

Music is a personal experience for every child. Once they learn the song, create a rhythm or relish a beat, it becomes part of their soul.

Carlos came into the classroom singing at the top of his lungs, "Ninety-nine bottles of beer on the wall, ninety-nine bottles of beer."

I started to sing with him and he stopped and looked at me and asks,

"Did my father teach you his song too?"

I responded, "He must have taught my father, because he use to sing that song to me when I was a child."

Carlos walked away and said, "Cool."

Tom Hunter, minstrel and music inter national educator said, "Teachers who enjoy music and sing with enthusiasm, regardless of ability or training, are the ones who receive the greatest response and involvement. Remember, you sing with children, not for them!"

BOOKS AND BOYS

Enticing some boys to look at books is no easy task. Many early childhood programs have chased boys away from books by making the experience of reading not natural for them. Asking boys to sit "Chris Cross, Apple Sauce," asking them to, "Use their quiet voice" during a story reading and "Sit Very Still" have all made boys dislike the whole reading experience. When reading and telling stories it is natural for boys to interrupt, ask questions, and pretend to be the characters in the book.

In one preschool program, I was called in as a consultant to work with boys who seemed to not show any interest in books or stories. I developed a strategy that worked very well called *Scoot A Story*. The procedure was that we took a book about frogs apart and laminated the pages. We taped the pages to the floor leaving every other space blank. The boys were told to look at the picture on one page and hop to the next blank one. They would then look at the next picture and hop again, until they were at the end of the pages.

Within three days we had boys very interested in books—looking at pictures, dictating to teachers about the pictures and creating their own stories. The boys, through moving rather then sitting, became very interested in reading and looking at books.

Scoot a Story

Move boys into action

Actions do speak louder their words. Boys are better at acting out stories compared to listening to them being read by a teacher or parent. They seem to comprehend the content of a book when they act it out with movement and gestures. Following are ways to actively engage boys with books:

- Allow boys to move during the reading or telling of a story
- Engage boys in dramatic play to demonstrate the story
- Provide boy-friendly culminating activities after completing books
- Read humorous books aloud
- Do not think that comic books are sub-literature
- Allow boys to participate in choosing books

Place appropriate books in centers

After reading the book *Tough Boris* by Mem Fox, the boys in my preschool started to make pirate movements that were in the book and repeating words like "massive," "scruffy," and "fearless"—all of which are difficult words to say and understand. As they started to act out the book, the words became more meaningful to the boys. They then went on to the art area to make pirate patches and added a whole new understanding of the book.

Placing books in each center with the cover visible, and a few pillows for sitting on encourages boys to "read on the go." Book or Reading centers are often areas where preschool children are expected to go select a book, and quietly sit down and look at it. This goes against the way boys are wired. Boys are not usually quiet and don't sit down to look at a book. This behavior doesn't fit their need to move and act out the book that they are reading. Boys are searching for books they like to look at and that fit their style of reading.

Jamie was in the block area, stacking blocks on top of each other. He yelled across the room, "I want to make an airplane!"

I went over to him, got down to his eye level and asked, "What do you need to build this airplane?"

Jamie responded, "I don't know."

I then gave him a suggestion, "Let's find a book that might have a picture of what kind of airplane you want to build." Jamie and I went over to the books that were in the block area and began to look for an airplane.

Jamie found one and yelled, "This is what I want to build!"

I read to him the kind of airplane it was and asked him to look around for what he thought he needed to build the one in the picture.

Jamie began to search for his material, which he worked with to make his airplane. Having the book available in the block area provided Jamie with some examples and content that supported his need for knowledge and better understanding of his project.

Books that are placed in the various centers, including the bathroom, should not reflect a theme or idea but the interests of the boys. Observe your group of children and find out what their interests are and then place books accordingly in the various centers.

Books in the bathroom center

Below is a beginning list of subjects of book categories and the centers they might fit in. Complete by adding centers and subject areas.

CENTER SUBJECT CHOICES	
Trucks, Community Helpers, Transportation	Block Center
Colors, Painting, Artists	Art Center
Sharks, Rocks, Nature	Science Center
Circus, Animals, Jungle	Large Motor Area
Numbers, Alphabet, Sewing	Fine Motor Area
Digging, Construction, Water	Sand/Water Area
Cooking, Recipes, Houses, Food Doctors, Teachers, Astronauts	Dramatic Play Area

Choose books for boys

A preschool teacher picked out the book *Rainbow Fish* to read at story time. Jeremy took a look at the book and yelled, "I don't want to read that girl book!"

Many boys get turned off to reading because of the selection of books available to them. *Rainbow Fish* is a terrific book about giving up scales to make other fish feel included. Most boys are not willing to give up scales. They are looking for the sharks who will eat other fish.

Many early childhood professionals have reported to me that boys have more reading difficulties than girls. Preschool boys spend very little time looking at books. Part of the reason for boys disinterest in books is the type of books available for them.

Sometimes boys use stories as a time to voice their fears, thoughts and feelings. A book that is "preachy," "teachy" or "cutesy" is better off not being used with boys. In most cases these types of books are not meaningful to boys and don't encourage conversations connected to their lives or imagination.

Every book that early childhood professionals read to children needs to create a desire in boys to want to be in the story. They must be allowed to change it to make it their own. Eventually boys create pictures in their brains. Remember the goal of reading or telling a story is not always to finish it, but to create opportunities for boys to own it.

I was reading a book, *The Boy Who Brought Home A Wave,* to a small cluster of children. The book describes a boy who loves waves at the beach so much that one day he brings one home with him.

I got to the page where he is home sleeping with the wave and Bret said, "You know, sometimes a wave comes to my bed."

"It does, how do you know?" I asked.

Bret said, "Sometimes, when I wake up in the morning the wave has left a wet spot on my sheet."

That led to lots of conversation about waves that have left wet spots on other children's beds too.

Books in the block center

CRITERIA FOR SELECTING BOOKS FOR BOYS

I have comprised this list for selecting books for boys:

- Does the book encourage acting it out?

- Do the pictures suggest movement?

- Are there action words?

- Do the pictures have less detail?

- Can boys identify with the main character?

- Does the book reflect different ages, races and abilities?

- Is there a beginning, middle and end to the story?

- Is the subject addressed in the book relevant to boys?

Recommended reading

The following are a few examples of books that have enticed boys.

Adventure:
- Simon, Seymour, *Seymour Simon's Book of Trains*
- Zane, Alexander, *The Wheels on the Race Car.*

Biography:
- De LA Hoya, Oscar, *Super Oscar*
- McDonough, Yona Zeldis, *Hammerin Hank: The Life of Hank Greenberg*

Fantasy/Science Fiction:
- Alexander, Martha, *I'll Protect You from the Jungle Beasts*
- Arnold, Tedd, *Parts*
- Arnold, Tedd, *Hi! Fly Guy*
- Barrett, Jodi, *Things That Are The Most*
- Fourde, Lynn, *The Pigs in the Mud*
- Maloney, Ted, *The Belly Button Boy*
- Mitton, Tony, *Down by the Cool of the Pool*

Folklore:
- Hamilton, Virginia, *Bruh Rabbit and the Tar Baby Girl*
- Kimmel, Eric, *The Runaway Tortilla*
- Palatini, Margie, *The Tree Silly Billies*
- Cuyler, Margery, *Skeleton Hiccups*
- Berkowitz Jacob, *Jurassic Poop*
- Fox, Mem, *Tough Boris*
- Ginsberg, Mira, *Clay Boy*
- Grossman, Bill, *My Little Sister Hugged an Ape*
- Grossman, Bill, *My Little Sister Ate One Hare*
- MacDonald, Elizabeth, *The Wolf is Coming*
- Reed, Lynn Rowe, *Please Don't Upset P.U. Zorilla!*
- Singer, Marilyn, *What Stinks?*

Humor:
- Feiffer, Jules, *Bark George*
- Downey, Lynn, *The Fleas Sneeze*
- Hort, Lenny, *The Seals on the Bus*
- Horsworth, Verner, *The Mole in Search of Who Done it*
- Munstean, Michaela, *Do Not Open This Book!*
- Palantini, Margie, *Bad Boys*
- Scienszka, Jon and Lane Smith, *The Stinky Cheese Man and Other Fairly Stupid Tales*
- Steig, William, *Pete's A Pizza*

Poetry
- Bryan, Ashley, *Let it Shine*
- Hopkins, Lee Bennett, *Oh, No! Where are My Pants? And Other Disaster Poems*
- Katz, Alan. *Take Me Out of the Bathtub and Other Silly Dilly Songs*

Writing on the Go

Writing in a preschool setting usually includes dictation by the teacher from the children, invented spelling, and labeling with words and pictures. Boys have not developed the same fine motor skills that girls have for handling writing utensils. Many boys will use their "fist" grasp when printing and will often need unlined larger sized paper. The following is what I have found that best encourages boys to write:

- Writing for boys usually includes standing up at a table rather than sitting down
- Boys write with fewer details or descriptions
- A larger space is needed for writing on
- Often boys writing relates to events that are current (within 5 minutes)
- Writing will usually involve some movement descriptions
- It is better to have writing utensils in all learning centers rather than a writing center. When a preschool setting has writing utensils in all centers the boy does not have to leave the center he is playing in to write a message he needs. If he has to go to the writing center, the likelihood is that he will not go and writing is discouraged.

Jimmy was in the block area and he said to me, "I don't want anyone to walk on my road" (a road he had made out of blocks).

My response, to encourage writing, was, "You will need to make a sign that says that." Jimmy went over to the block shelf and picked up a piece of paper and pencil and wrote, "Kept Of." Jimmy then taped it to his road.

I not only encouraged block play, but also writing. If I had told Jimmy to go to the writing center and make a sign, it probably would not have happen for fear that someone would take his road.

Boys and girls are wired differently for dictation skills. When you look at Missy's dictation letter, observe how detailed she is in describing how to ride a bike.

Missy's Story

First you get on your bicycle and put your one hand on the bar.

And you put your other hand on the other bar.

Then you put your one foot on the pedal, and your other foot on the other peddle. And then you put your butt on the seat.

Now you know how to ride a bike.

If you did not know how to ride a bicycle, with Missy's detailed description you most likely could. Her thoughts were organized and her details were clear.

Boys approach writing and dictation differently. Kevin is five years of age. Look at what Kevin has to say about Little Red Riding Hood:

Kevin's Story

Once upon a time, there was a little girl name Little Red Riding Hood.

No one knew why she walked, she should be riding something.

The next morning my teacher asked Little Red Riding Hood,

"Why are you always walking?"

This gave Little Red Riding Hood an idea.

She went to a Toyota Factory to buy a car, but didn't like anything there.

So she then went to a bike place.

She liked a bike and bought one.

Now Red Riding Hood rides.

Notice Kevin's letter has fewer details and he is concerned about the action of Little Red Riding Hood. "Why is she walking, she should be riding something?"

For dictation purposes, asking boys questions that relate to movement or action will encourage them to make up stories and attempt to write them down. The following questions might be asked:

- In the block area – "What do you need to do to make your house, road, etc.?"
- In the art area – "How did you paint that picture?"
- In the house area – "Show me how you made that soup?"
- At snack time – "How do you think you milk a cow to get that glass of milk you are drinking?"

To encourage boys to write, having pencils and/or ink pens, paper, and tape in all centers will result in more writing attempts. If the utensils are in sight they will make writing a part of their daily experiences wherever they are playing.

Math—It's Not Just Counting

Joel, a preschool child, came up to me and looked at my shoes. He then responded with, "Wow, your feet are giants!"

I said to Joel, "Yes I do have big shoes."

He took his foot and put it beside mine and responded, "My feet are a lot smaller then yours."

I said, "You're right, my feet are bigger than yours."

Joel then paused and looked at me. He then smiled and said, "You can kill a lot of ants can't you?"

Math for boys is everywhere, including the size of your feet and how many ants you could kill.

Mathematics, like science, is a subject that boys at one time excelled in. In the past 10 years there hasn't been the same cognitive growth evidence. What happened?

As I looked at math training literature I noticed that math experiences for young children have moved from the hands-on learning mode to the critical thinking mode. Both are important areas for mathematical learning. The difference is that boys are not often wired to discuss how they achieved an answer as much as showing you what they did. In time boys can learn the critical thinking process. Without the "real" active experiences of manipulating materials first, boys cannot easily analyze or report their conclusions. Providing everyday natural experiences will help boys practice seriation, conservation and other important math skills.

Here are some simple and active math experiences for boys:

Plastic Bag Poke

Materials:

- Small plastic bags
- Twist ties
- Pencils
- Water
- Plastic tub

Explore by:

- Filling the sandwich bags with water. Gathering the top of the bag and sealing with twist ties or rubber bands.
- Holding the bag by the top and pushing a pencil completely through both sides of the bag. You will probably want to hold the bag over a plastic tub.
- Seeing how many pencils they can push into the bag. It won't leak.

Pipe Insulation Speeds

Materials:

- Pipe insulation
- Marbles
- Plastic golf balls

Explore by:

- Cutting the pipe insulation in half lengthwise to create tracks.
- Having the boys put marbles or golf balls on the track. They will see how to make the balls build speed by how they hold the track.
- Practicing fast and slow speeds.

Velcro Ball Toss

Materials:
- Velcro tape
- Different sized balls

Explore by:
- Taking different size balls and wrapping Velcro tape around them.
- Putting Velcro strips on a flat surface.
- Throwing balls to see how many they can get to attach to the Velcro strips.

Measuring

Materials:
- Measuring tapes
- Rulers
- Yardsticks
- Paper
- Pencils

Explore by:
- Taking the different measuring materials and going around the classroom, inside and out, measuring objects.
- Writing down measurements with pencils and paper.

Blocks for Math

Blocks provide the most important opportunity for boys to practice emerging math skills. They learn balancing, sorting, patterning, classification, seriation and counting. Boys need to move things, build them up and knock them down and fit things into different spaces.

The following is a simple list of different types of blocks:
- Hollow Blocks
- Spools
- Lincoln logs
- Dr. Drew's Blocks
- Tree Blocks
- Duplos
- Waffle blocks

Jimmy, a preschool child, was building with wooden blocks. Every time he got to a particular point in his building the blocks tumbled down. Jimmy would gather the blocks and build them up again. Each time the block tower would tumble down before he wanted them to. I watched with amazement on how

Dr. Drew's Blocks

many attempts that Jimmy made, thinking he was going to give up any minute.

Jimmy started to build with the blocks again, but this time stopped to looked at what he had accomplished so far. He turned two blocks around and added another block. He continued to build his block tower and they didn't fall down. When he was finished, he stood back and looked at his tower.

Smiling, he turned to the teacher and said, "It needed more blocks to keep it up."

He quickly learned that building takes some form of mathematical practice.

Boys with blocks

COMPUTERS AND BOYS—EARLY ISN'T ALWAYS BETTER

The computer, like the TV, can be a mesmerizing babysitter. The volume of data and flashy special effects of the World Wide Web and lots of other software overwhelm many children, especially boys. Many boys have trouble focusing on more then one task at a time. Many computer programs make the boy's brain swirl, bombarding it with many acts of violence and chaos. Boys who are exposed to computers can alarmingly become deficient in generating their own images and ideas.

Creativity and imagination are prerequisites for innovative thinking, which will never be obsolete. Most technology in school today will be obsolete long before the five-year-old graduates.

The body and the brain are connected, especially for boys. Movement is needed to connect all the senses. You simply can't get this through the TV or computers. The promise to have computers in all preschool classrooms scares me. If there is room for computers that means there is more room for blocks. Do computers really "connect" boys to the real world? Too often, what computers actually connect children to are trivial games, aggressive advertising and isolation. These experiences are the opposite of what boys need, especially those boys who are at risk of not developing close relationships with caring adults.

I watched a young boy in a preschool classroom at a computer. What fascinated me was the amount of time he stared at the screen without saying a word to anyone. The software he was engaged with asked him to make choices and decisions and would tell him if his answers were right or wrong by a green GO sign for yes and a red STOP sign for no. He spent around twenty minutes doing this computer activity. With boys already lagging in language development, he never was encouraged to talk during the whole computer activity.

I asked myself, "What is the benefit of this experience? Is it to keep him quiet and isolated from others?" Let's bring back the "real world" of play and help boys grow into thinking, talking, and relationship building. There will be lots of time for boys to get involved with computers as they mature, both physically and cognitively.

In this chapter, I touch on a few examples of activities that support the healthy "wiring" of boys' brains. These activities are offered in the spirit of my belief about the qualities of boys that we need to support; a serious passion for learning, a desire to make changes, and an eagerness to take risks. As early childhood professionals we can keep reminding ourselves that the curriculum works best when it comes from the child. Our job is to become careful observers of boys and how they respond to the climate we set up for them. Only in this way can we determine whether we are asking boys to make potentially harmful changes in their lives or supporting their development in positive and lasting ways.

4 The Hard Parts

When we forget about the differences between boys and girls presented in Chapter 1 of this book, we set ourselves up for daily frustrations in early childhood settings. Following are some of the most common questions that educators ask me. In my answers you'll find many suggestions for solving problems and preventing conflict.

HOW CAN I MODEL EFFECTIVE BEHAVIOR FOR BOYS?

In a preschool setting, David was sitting at the snack table finishing his food. When done, he got up and started to walk away. The teacher said to David, "David, if you are done, put your paper products in the trash."

David ignored her and went to the block area.

The teacher walked over to David, took his hand, and said, "If you don't pick up your paper and throw it away in the trash, you will not get to play." She started to walk him towards the snack table.

David pulled away and yelled, "You can't make me, You're not my mom."

The teacher said, "I don't care if I am not your mom. In our school you have to pick up your paper and put it in the trash."

Is David being defiant? Or is this just not the moment to take on the issue of throwing paper away? I am not suggesting that picking up after yourself is a goal to ignore. But I am wondering if it was crucial for David to learn at that very moment.

It doesn't help that adults convey anger and resentment to children, as illustrated in this incident with David. Adults frequently talk down to boys, making demands and modeling rudeness. Children are often treated in ways that adults would not treat each other.

As teachers, we must remind ourselves that *how* we respond to a conflict is more important than finding an immediate solution. What we say and how we say it are being observed not only by the child at the center of conflict but also by the whole classroom.

When boys don't understand the immediate need for some event to occur, they are frequently perceived as being rude and impolite. However, it's important to put their responses in the context of what we know about brain development, as discussed in Chapter 1. A statement such as *pick up your toys so that you don't fall on them when you are walking* assumes that connections are immediate. In reality, the connections can fail. The boy may not see the natural consequence of leaving toys or paper strewn around a room. In turn, he might be labeled defiant or mean, especially if he responds to a teacher's command by simply tossing the toys or trash into a different area.

Faced with situations like these, we can become better models for boys in two ways. First, we can change what we say. The chart on page 75 offers some examples.

Second, we can change what we do. Actions truly speak louder than words. During conflicts, help boys to recognize visual cues and behave in new ways. Boys need many opportunities to practice gestures and facial expressions that boost their social interaction. For example, teachers commonly respond to an angry boy by saying, "Tell them how you feel." This is less productive than saying, "When you cross your arms across your chest" (demonstrate the movement), "it tells other children to back off. Is that what you want?"

Here are a few more examples of action demonstration:

- When you raise your fist, that shows other children you are going to hit them (demonstrate the fist formation).
- When you cover your ears (demonstrate by putting your hands over your ears), you let others know you don't want to listen.
- When you raise your leg like this (demonstrate a kicking motion), you let others know you are going to kick them.
- When you throw the blocks (demonstrate a throwing gesture), it tells other children you don't want them by you.

Early childhood professionals who want to prevent conflicts often choose to simply forbid certain activities. Instead, I encourage you to ask, "How can I make sure a positive experience happens?" rather than "Should I permit this experience at all?"

During one of my presentations, for example, a teacher asked this question, "If I allow children to walk up the slide, won't it open up more conflicts, especially to children who are coming down the slide?" My response to this quite realistic question is to demonstrate the desired action. Make sure that the children who are going up the slide first ask, "Is anyone coming down the slide?"

If we want to assist boys in developing self-control, then we as the adults in his life are going to need to make most of the changes. In summary, what you can do to help is:

- Describe what you *want* a child to do instead of what you *don't* want.
- Role-play conflicts and solutions.
- Remember that sometimes boys give orders and sometimes speak in louder voices—and ignore these behaviors as often as possible.
- Provide solitary spaces ("caves") for boys to enter and cool down.
- Provide opportunities for safe roughhousing.
- Relate the display of empathy to a physical task.
- Use lots of visual guidance, such as posting signs that say *stop*.

The left-hand column of the chart below lists some examples of what parents and educators typically say to boys who are "in trouble." The right-hand column offers some more effective responses (with blanks for you to fill in as appropriate):

EFFECTIVE RESPONSES	
Instead of saying . . .	*Say . . .*
We don't hit our friends.	Let me show you what to hit.
No running.	Run on the tape over there.
We share our toys.	When you finish with this, make sure ____ gets it.
We don't call our friends names.	His name isn't _____. It is _____
Use your words.	Tell him you want it.
Make a better choice.	Tell him: It is hard for me to wait for that truck, and that is why I hit.
We don't say, 'I hate you.'	What do you want that he has?
Use your inside voice.	Alice, move away from him. He likes to use his louder voice.
No spinning with those beads.	Stand back, he likes to spin.
No pushing.	Did you ask if she wants to be pushed?
We don't play guns.	Did you ask if he wanted to play?

How Can I Get Aggressive Boys to Stop Hitting?

When I asked early childhood professionals, from across the country, why boys are being removed from preschool, I discovered that the top five causes were hitting, biting, pushing, swearing, and defiance. Teachers often report that boys tend to be more aggressive than girls. Reasons for this might include testosterone spikes that happen during the day and that boys often demonstrate "caring" in different ways than girls do.

Solutions to aggressive behavior begin with the insight that *not all-aggressive behavior is negative*. When a boy pushes another child out of the way to get to the toy that he wants, remember that he is still a natural egocentric child. He simply may fail to notice that there is another child who wants to play with the same toy. He may not understand that someone can get hurt after getting knocked down to the floor.

Preventing aggressive behavior means creating an environment that promotes self-control. This environment helps boys recognize that there are choices to make and that they are in control of their decisions. Such insights do not come easily for boys, especially when they are placed in an environment that forces them to care about others first. Boys need to be around teachers who model empathy and send the message: *I know you wish you could have this toy first. I wish you could, too. What are you going to do, while you wait until he is done with it?* This reflects the boy's need to have the toy and states that it is not going to always happen right now. Boys need to be around teachers who also send this message: *I know you are mad and you want to hit him. Since you are so mad, I am going to find something for you to hit.* This allows the boy to realize that anger is natural—and can be redirected.

A no-hitting rule creates an expectation for boys that is too high. It assumes that boys won't ever hit. Wrong! They need to hit, push, and shove—and to do these things often. The issue is not how to get boys to stop hitting. The question is: What *can* they hit?

When tempers between two boys flare and one of them hits the other, first ask the boy who was hit, "Do you want to be hit?" If his response is no, then make sure he states this fact loudly to the boy who did the hitting. You can

STEPS FOR REDUCING HITTING WITH BOYS

1. Take the boy's hands firmly.

2. Ask the child who is being hit, "Do you want his hand in your _____?"

3. Ask the child who is being hit to say loudly, "Stop hitting my _____."

4. Give the child who is doing the hitting something that he *can* hit.

5. Say to the hitter, "Because you want to hit, hit this hard! This you can hit a lot!"

help by restating the point, "He doesn't want to be knocked down." Then take the hand of the hitter and find something else for him to hit, such as a cardboard box or pillow. Then say, "Hit this whenever you feel like hitting. Now hit it hard." Stay with the boy as he continues to hit the box, and remember that you will have to remind him of this often.

Providing objects for boys to hit, push, and shove can defuse boys' motivation to hit their peers.

WHAT CAN I DO WITH A BULLY?

Abdul yelled at John, "You can't play with us."

John said, "Yes I can. You don't own the school."

Abdul yelled, "We won't let you play with us, so go away."

John walked away.

Many teachers would immediately think that Abdul is a bully. Yet we have to ask ourselves: At this stage of development, is he a bully—or a child trying to find his own sense of power?

Many boys at the preschool level are exploring the subject of domination. They see it demonstrated in movies and television, and it might be modeled at home. Our culture is filled with messages that life is better when we acquire power over people.

Before you can recognize that others are important, you first have to develop a strong sense of self. For boys, this development often means playing domination roles, such as games that involve locking robbers up in jail or putting out fires to save the school. At these times, boys give orders to other children and practice using a louder, firmer voice.

The child we often need to assist during "bullying" is not the one doing the bullying but the one who is being bullied. When we teach the targets of bullying to be strong, confident and in control, we prevent bullying. When you don't have victims, then you don't have bullies.

The following are some simple techniques for working with a child who gets bullied:

- Model how to say *no* loud and firmly.
- Help the child practice putting his hand up to protect his space.
- Help the child get power by being heard.
- Remind the child to ask for adult help if needed.

Also remember that both boys and girls can be bullies. We often notice boys who bully because of the obvious physical evidence. However, girls often bully by calling names or telling stories about each other. This is hurtful, even when the consequences are not noticed right away.

HOW CAN I AVOID GETTING INTO POWER STRUGGLES WITH BOYS?

Lee was sitting at the snack table using his spoon to stir juice. His teacher said, "Stop stirring your juice with your spoon. You will end up spilling it!"

The other children looked at Lee. He hit his juice cup with the spoon and knocked it over.

The teacher said to Lee, "You cannot have anymore more juice if you are going to spill it."

"I don't want any of that yucky juice anyhow," Lee replied with a laugh.

The other children laughed with him.

"Lee, get up from the table and go look at a book until the rest of us finish," the teacher said.

Who won that power struggle? I am going to bet on Lee.

Boys are sensitive to the feeling of shame. They will almost do anything to avoid that feeling, even if it means hurting someone else. Their body and soul tells them to avoid failure at all costs.

For boys, the shame is often linked to the experience of failure. Yet many early childhood professionals unconsciously promote failure by:

- Asking boys to use their "inside voice"
- Asking boys to use their "walking feet"
- Planning experiences that have competition
- Making boys stand in line
- Asking boys to take turns
- Asking boys to share
- Expecting boys to act like "little adults"

When we put boys in situations that lead to feelings of failure, they will look for ways to achieve power. The easiest way to meet this goal is through a power struggle. All a boy has to do is make his teacher/parent upset and he feels like a winner. Many boys begin to think that the only way they can feel successful is to get adults involved in power struggles.

During the incident described above, the teacher could have said, "Lee, I noticed that you like to stir your juice with a spoon. Let me find a place that you can do that." Lee would remain with his feelings of power and probably would have stopped the stirring at the snack table.

Better yet, why not just ignore the stirring of the juice?

The box below is to assist you in making better responses to actions that push your buttons.

WHAT PUSHES YOUR BUTTONS?

Button Pushers	*Best Responses*
1. Whining, "He hit me!"	1. "Did you tell him to stop?"
2.	2.
3.	3.
4.	4.
5.	5.
6.	6.
7.	7.
8.	8.
9.	9.
10.	10.

Is the time-out chair an effective strategy for boys?

My observation of time-out chairs in preschool settings is that the same boys are always sitting in them. Perhaps this is an indication that the strategy is not working.

Time-out chairs were originally developed to give a child a break from the stress and pressure of the environment—not as a tool for punishment. Boys who are placed in a time-out chair are probably not thinking about what they did wrong. Instead, they are thinking about what they can do once they get off the chair.

My observations on the use of time-out chairs do not provide much evidence that they work. The longer a boy sits in a time-out chair, the more his brain will seek protection by going into pause state (see Chapter 1 for an explanation of this term). And, no learning takes place during a pause state. Time-out chairs are often vehicles of public recognition for "bad" behavior. Remember that boys are often looking for recognition. So how do boys receive recognition for "good" behavior?

How can I deal with roughhousing?

I offer some basic answers to this question in Chapter 2. Here I will expand on those ideas and offer additional strategies.

Remember when you were a child and played the game Red Rover, Red Rover Send (insert your name) Right Over? As you were running over, you did not yell, "I'm coming but I'll be gentle." No! Instead, you ran as fast as you could until you broke the chain of hands. Sometimes you even used your whole body to slam into the chain and cause many children to fall down.

In our culture, how has Red Rover, Red Rover come to be classified as a violent game? In many preschools, this results from a "zero tolerance" policy. My experience tells me that Red Rover and other games based on physical movement actually help boys who are in the middle of a testosterone spike become *less* violent.

Roughhousing needs to be brought back to preschool. This does *not* mean allowing children to re-create World Wide Wrestling. It *does* mean finding ways for boys and girls to play in positive and physically active ways.

What do I mean by roughhousing? There are several possible answers. For one, it is physical. It can range from a hug or handshake to rough-and-tumble play. It often takes the form of games that allow children the pleasure of testing their own strength. For boys, in most cases, it is non-verbal, common during a testosterone spike, and quite nurturing. Roughhousing is also a voluntary activity—one that children can enter and leave as they wish. Most importantly, there is no correlation between roughhousing and violence.

Even infant boys will show more assertive movements than girls. They pull harder, kick their legs more vigorously, crawl with vigor, and throw food on the floor. Testosterone spikes can fuel such behaviors as early as six month of age. All these can be seen as early forms of roughhousing.

There are several types of roughhousing that you can include in preschool:

- *Running into boxes.* Go to the appliance store and pick up large cardboard boxes, such as those used for refrigerators and stoves. When a boy demonstrates the need to hit, take him over to one of these boxes and say, "Hit this real hard, because you like to hit."
- *Running through newspapers.* Ask two adults or children to hold on to an open sheet of newspaper. Ask children to run through the newspaper, ripping it into pieces. Sometimes it helps if you encourage children to scream as they run through.
- *Climbing.* Remember as a child when you would climb to the top of a hill, or to the top of a slide. You felt all the power in the world. With this in mind, buy or build ladders, preferably five- or six-feet high, for your preschool classroom. Place mats under the ladders and, with adult supervision, allow the children to climb to the top.
- *Tug of war.* Get a rope, tie it around your waist, and yell "Tug of war!" Allow children to grab the rope and try to pull you over. This seems to work well on days when children present lots of behavioral challenges.
- *Handshaking.* I like to greet the children every morning with the words, "I've been waiting for you." During this greeting, I shake their hands. With boys I shake their hands so hard that their whole body moves up and down.
- *High fives.* Rather than giving verbal praise, when a boy needs encouragement, allow him to jump up and slap your hands.
- *Rough and tumble.* Get down on the floor and allow children to jump on you. This is even better when you invite parents and guardians to take on your role. Boys and girls love this. If a child raises his hand in a fist motion, avoid saying "No boxing." Instead, say "Stop—take that hand and wrap it around my arm" (or leg).

I worry that boys will suffer without an outlet for physical play. Roughhousing is important to boys' social development but often misinterpreted as aggression. At around age five, boys start to feel uncomfortable showing affection through touch. Rough and Tumble play may let boys express intimacy in a safe, acceptable way. Again, remember that each child freely chooses when to join—and when to leave—roughhousing.

WHAT CAN I DO ABOUT BOYS WHO WANT TO PLAY GUNS OR SWORDS?

When my daughter was a preschooler, my wife and I made sure that she wasn't exposed to "violence" on television: no pretend guns, and certainly no form of corporal punishment.

When she was four years old, we had a party. Our daughter's job was to answer the door with excitement. This was her choice, and we respected her decision.

When the first doorbell rang, our daughter turned the knob, opened the door, and smiled. At that point our precious non-violent child raised her hand aimed her pointer finger at the guest, and said, "Bang! I got you. You're dead." The same thing happened with every ring of the doorbell.

My wife and I looked at each other in shock. What could we have done to create such a "violent" child?

As I thought about it all night, I began to realize what she was saying with her action was *Come on in, but this is my territory*—not *I want to kill you.*

Children (especially boys) turn many things into guns or swords—including but not limited to fingers, blocks, paper, and even toast. As with roughhousing, children usually do not play guns or swords because they want to hurt or kill. Through this kind of play boys are not saying: "I'm practicing to be a killer." Instead, they play with guns and swords because using these objects can create tremendous feelings of power and control. I have found that the more opportunity for children to gain power and control in a classroom, the less likely they will play guns and swords.

Zero Tolerance policies sprang up around the country after the Columbine High School Shootings in 1999. Nervous school officials, worried about liability issues, soon began to apply policies about guns and other toys that treated even the most minor violation as a cause for expulsion.

Millions of men in this country who played with toy guns or swords as children did not grow up to become serial killers

Being a toy-weapon-tolerant parent doesn't mean I'm thrilled by gunplay. I would prefer that boys play nation-builder or rocket scientist. However, before they get to such fantasies, children seem to work out more basic emotions in more basic ways.

What I say to children when they pretend to shoot me is, "I don't play that game. You will need to ask someone who wants to." No moralizing at this stage—just respectful solutions. If children pretend to shoot another child and that child screams out *no*, I go to the child who is doing the shooting and say, "Did you ask first if they wanted to play that game?" This is more effective than saying:

- We don't shoot our friends. (He will then only shoot children he doesn't like.)
- Shooting hurts. (That is not true when you are pretending.)
- You can squirt flowers but you cannot shoot him. (What is so powerful about squirting flowers?)
- The rule in our school is no shooting. (Children might not understand what a rule is until much later in their development.)

Many preschool teachers seem to be concerned about swordplay. This can be another activity that represents how powerful children feel. Children commonly practice this form of play during their testosterone spikes. Testosterone influences power and control. Trying to teach boys to rise above gunplay or swordplay and be more sensitive without first teaching them acceptable ways to use their physical energy spikes will often fail. The results can include even more boys who have social and emotional problems. Boys will not trust a teacher or their environment if their needs are not supported.

However, as an educator you can offer gun and swordplay, that maintain safety and respect, while providing children with lots of fun. Try this: Go to a discount store and purchase swimming "noodles," those long colorful Styrofoam tubes. Cut these in half and place them in a box. If you have that day when "all hell breaks loose," simply shout, *"Sword fight!"* Ask the children to grab the noodles, yell, "On *Guard*" and swing the noodles at each other. They will feel all the power in the world—and no one will get hurt.

Will "super hero" play promote violence?

I remember playing Superman when I was very young. Wearing my cape, I raced around the room yelling "I'm faster than a speeding bullet!" I really thought I was the strongest man in the world, and no one could tell me otherwise.

As they do with gunplay, children imitate super hero characters because it creates feelings of power. Even so, there is no evidence that playing superhero causes violent behavior. My observations indicate that allowing superhero play actually decreases children's need to gain power by pushing and shoving.

There might be other benefits as well. Paley explains that boys who are involved in super hero play interact more positively with adults and feel a sense of belonging in a group. (Paley, 1984, 67)

Also consider that super hero play can help boys:

- Learn differences between good and bad, power and vulnerability, and rules and control.

Super hero cape

- Control their fears by repeatedly "trying on" power.
- Develop problem-solving skills.
- Gain social skills.
- Develop physically as they jump, run, and imitate other traits of their heroes.

During super hero play, boys will run more and sometimes want to be more dominant. Keep in mind that a boy's need to dominate will depend greatly on whether he perceives himself as physically weak or lacking in control.

Early childhood professionals can provide ongoing guidance to reinforce the "guardrails" needed for this kind of activity. I suggest the following props to support super hero play:

- *Capes.* You can easily make these from old drapes or curtains. Add Velcro so children can latch their capes. Velcro is safe because it will immediately detach if caught on something. Add capes to the "house" area of your classroom.
- *Nets.* These allow the boys to chase the "horrible monsters" that hide in the deep, dark sea. Purchase inexpensive fish netting.
- *Pirate eye patches.* Every boy wants to be a pirate! Patches can be made out of cloth. Attach elastic to go around the head.
- *Fire hoses.* Take old garden hoses and cut them in lengths of about four feet. Hang these on the walls in spots that are low enough for the boys to reach when someone yells out a pretend fire.

How can I respond to boys who use loud voices?

Cory and David were going around the classroom pretending to chain-saw table legs, chairs, easels, and even some of the other children. At the same time, they were using their loud voices to make chain-saw noises.

The teacher went up to them and said, "We only have inside chain-saws at our school. You will have to lower your sound."

The boys looked at her and began to use loud voices again. Again the teacher reminded the boys to "Use an inside chain-saw voice." They did not stop but laughed and raised their volume even more. Finally the teacher said, "If you don't stop making those loud chain-saw noises, you will not be able to go outside." This threat stopped the "chain-sawing."

However, I can't help but wonder what would happen if this teacher went to a hardware store and told the sales clerk that she would like to by an "inside chain-saw." Would she be able to find one? The only chain-saws I've ever heard are loud and boisterous. And that's what Cory and David were demonstrating.

It is no surprise that boys tend to speak at higher volumes in the preschool classroom. Boys like the louder parts of songs and scream, without hesitation, "John, come over here, see what I have." They could be right next to you and scream, "I have to go PEE!"

A common statement made by teachers in a preschool setting is "Use your inside voice." In response, boys might simply offer a loud reply, "I am using my inside voice!" Asking boys to use their quiet voice or whisper is like asking them to "die." Being loud is like flipping an "on" switch for their brain. It helps boys become more alert. Perhaps preschool teachers actually need to say "Use a louder voice."

Preschool teachers have reported to me that male teachers can get boys to respond better to them than female teachers. I find no evidence for this statement. But I have found that boys respond more readily to louder, firmer voices—the kind of voices that male teachers tend to use when disciplining children. If female teachers used louder and firmer voices, then they might get a similar response from boys.

If you have low tolerance with loud boys, the best solution is to purchase earplugs or ear muffs. Offer these to children who hold their ears because the boys are being too loud.

How can I help boys listen more effectively?

During my observations in preschool settings, I noticed the following differences between boys and girls:

- Girls often would hear more of what the teacher said.
- Girls many times were better at following oral directions.
- Girls usually gave feedback immediately.
- Boys often heard fewer details that were given.
- Boys looked for visual reminders.
- Boys needed directions given with a beginning, middle, and end.

To help boys listen when they need to organize tasks, give directions that have a clear beginning, middle, and end. In preschool classrooms, for example, teachers often announce that, "In five more minutes, it will be time to clean up." Boys frequently ignore this statement. Part of the reason is that most of them are visual and not auditory learners. Another reason is that the statement does not have a beginning, middle, and end format. What helps boys are instructions such as these:

- *Beginning*: When I show this poster with five dots...
- *Middle*: It will be time to put the toys on the shelves with the matching pictures...
- *End*: So we can walk outside and play with your favorite toy.

Kenneth Horn notes that "boys prune information from the brain within five minutes unless it is real (related to action), relevant to them, and hooked to an emotion" (MiAEYC Presentation, 2003). I worry about how much information is being "poured" into boys' brains—only to quickly disappear. For example, why do we spend so much time on teaching preschool children about the calendar? How is this real, relevant and hooked to an emotion? Why does a child under five need to know the current day, month and year? What are they going to do with this information?

When the information that we give does not meet Dr. Horn's criteria, then boys will have to relearn it over and over again. The only relevant, real, and hooked-to-an-emotion day for a boy under age five is his birthday—which he claims is often, because he has not developed knowledge of time.

If we want boys to develop language skills—reading, writing, and listening—then we must include many relevant, action-based activities in the preschool setting. The decision not to make these changes will only channel more boys into programs for students who are delayed in these areas.

HOW CAN I HELP BOYS DEVELOP HEALTHY EMOTIONAL BONDS?

Our brain—the organ that allows us to see, smell, taste, think, talk and move—is also the organ that allows us to love. Certain areas of the brain help us to form and maintain emotional relationships, and these areas are in active development during the first years of life. Experiences during this early period, when children are especially vulnerable, are critical to inhibiting aggression and developing a host of other characteristics displayed by healthy, happy, and productive human beings.

Most mental health specialists define *attachment* as a special and enduring kind of emotional relationship with a specific person. Core attachment capabilities are formed during infancy. Healthy attachment with a primary caregiver appears to be associated with a high probability of healthy relationships. Without predictable, responsive nurturing and sensory-enriched care giving, a child's potential for normal bonding and attachments will not be realized.

Bonding-related behaviors are different for boys than for girls. For boys, the important factor is positive physical contact: rocking, jumping, bouncing, and roughhousing. These activities lead to positive emotional attachments.

Our brain's "wiring" for healthy relationships depends on having the right kinds of experiences at the right points in life. Timing is everything. Bonding experiences lead to healthy attachments and healthy capabilities when they are provided in the earliest years of life.

Early childhood professionals are now playing a key role in attachment and bonding. A larger percent of children are placed in programs outside of their home. When parents are working or going to school, an early childhood professional can become a key person in the development of attachment and bonding.

The "fit" between early childhood professionals and infant boys is crucial. Some professionals are just fine with a calm infant but overwhelmed by an infant who moves a lot or is frustrated easily. The results—which might include impaired bonding—can be devastating. Boys without stimulation and nurturing can literally lose the capacity to form meaningful relationships that impact the rest of their lives.

You can do several things to promote healthy bonding.

- Provide consistency in caregivers. This is essential, especially for boys. Their brains struggle with changes in the team of adults who care for them. Behavioral challenges increase when the size of the group increases.

- Provide consistency in activities as well. Boys need a stable daily routine, so avoid major changes in the schedule. Remember the *Mister Rogers Show*? He always entered his home and took off his outside shoes and blazer, replacing them with tennis shoes and a more casual sweater. These actions said to the viewers: *We are now starting the program.* Young boys thrive with ordered routine such as this one. When boys know what to expect, they can make choices that promote learning.

- Offer regular opportunities for appropriate physical connection. Simple roughhousing and "high fives" can be used for this purpose. So can silly songs that make children smile:

Everybody knows that I love my toes,
Everybody knows that I love my toes.
I love my ears, my eyes, my tongue and my nose.
But everybody knows that I love my toes.

- Keep the staff-child ratio high and the class size low. Boys need enough caregivers to go around. Boys generally have more difficulty adapting and changing when stress is present in the classroom.

Following are additional tips for helping boys develop the brain structures that lead to healthy attachment:

- Call boys by their name ("honey" only comes in a bottle or jar).

- Learn about your boys' worlds—the specifics about what they like and don't like.

- Sing songs often, knowing that children don't care about the quality of your voice.

- Avoid making judgments ("quiet" does not necessarily mean "better").

- Touch in subtle ways—for example, by taking a small, soft brush and lightly brushing a child's skin.

- Encourage the child to move often by stretching, rolling, climbing.

- Smile, remembering that this provides immediate, positive feedback.

Should we have single sex classrooms?

During the workshops that I present across the country, the most common question from my audiences is, "Should we educate boys and girls separately?" My immediate response is, "No, not in early childhood settings."

Imagine what could happen to these environments if we dropped the policy of treating boys and girls as if they are the same. We would create classrooms where boys can get special verbal and language training. We could give girls more help in mastering areas of the curriculum that involve spatial concepts. In short, we need environments that support children's different needs—not separate classrooms.

Much of what children learn in early childhood settings results from their modeling of each other. Girls model verbal abilities, caring, empathy, and the need to work in groups. Boys model physical abilities, power, drive, and the need for some solitary play. The kind of teachers boys and girls need can sometimes be loud, dramatic, and extroverted—and sometimes quiet, kindly, and subdued.

Education can never be gender neutral. Boys and girls are simply too different. We can continue to ignore these differences. Or we can create lessons designed for boys' brains and lessons for girls' brains, applying the latest research and observations on gender differences to our daily work in the classroom.

Boys' Behaviors can be both challenging and exiting. This chapter raises several questions that discuss the "hard parts" of being an early childhood professional. Many teachers, when addressing guidance and discipline issues, attempt to become more controlling of boys' actions. They often set up rules that tell children what they can't do, hoping that the behavior they view as negative will change or stop. Rules that say "No" frequently stimulate negative behaviors and create lots of opportunities for boys to involve adults in power struggles. The following list of New Rules for Boys state what behaviors are natural for boys and need to be encouraged.

NEW RULES FOR BOYS THAT WORK BETTER IN EARLY CHILDHOOD SETTINGS

 Run here often

 Climb higher

 Build higher

 Go up the slide

 Use outside voices inside

 Be silly often

 Hit boxes harder

 Sing loud

 Push this

 Be a "Blood Thirsty" Pirate

 Dig to China

 Be messy

 Knock down the blocks

 Use lots

 Only listen when it is relevant to you

5 Success Stories

Arick the "hitter"

When Arick first came to my program, I wondered if he would ever stop hitting other children. He hurt so much inside. The need for hurting others was a release from his own pain.

Arick came from a home where both parents worked. He had four brothers and sisters, and he spent eight to ten hours each weekday in childcare. He didn't receive much positive recognition at home, either. By the time he arrived, there was only enough time for the parents to assist the younger siblings, get dinner ready, and complete other daily tasks. As Arick's first year in childcare progressed, his hitting of other children increased.

I carefully observed the strategies used by early childhood professionals as they responded to Arick's behavior. They tried to reason with him: "We can't hit other children because it hurts them." Adults would get down at Arick's eye level and make sure that they made eye contact when talking to him. Then they would sit with Arick at a table and assist him with an activity.

On the surface, all of this looked fine. But after further observation I noticed that Arick usually hit children when he was angry, or when one of the early childhood professionals was close by. I concluded that what Arick wanted was something basic—an acknowledgement that he existed.

I met with the staff that worked with Arick, and we decided to use a different strategy. Our conclusion was that Arick did not receive recognition in his busy home. In addition, he got no recognition during childcare unless he hit. This was why his hitting increased.

When Arick arrived at the center the next morning, someone immediately acknowledged him. Also, throughout the day, adults asked him to do things and he was acknowledged for responding, "Arick, would you show Carol how you put that puzzle together? She is having some difficulty." This continued for at least three more weeks.

One day I was standing close to Arick and he looked at me and said, "I am not going to hit anyone today, because my heart is not hurting anymore." He finally felt a sense of belonging. I went home crying that night, knowing that I hadn't given up.

DAMEON THE "BOMBER"

Dameon, four years old, attended a preschool center. He was continually throwing blocks at children in the classroom. His parents knew that soon they were going to be asked to pull him out. They called and ask if I might be able to help with Dameon's behavior, since the preschool was not having any success.

I visited the preschool program and spent two days watching Dameon's routine. He spent most of his time in the block area. He would build tall structures and stand back and look at his accomplishments. Everything was okay until children would come into the block area and begin to build their own structures. He would pick up blocks and throw them at children yelling, "Bombs away." This continued until children either left the block space or cried from being hit. This behavior would continue throughout the preschool day.

The preschool teachers would go up to Dameon and say to him, "You will need to leave the block area, because we can't throw blocks. They will hurt our friends." Dameon would scream, "I don't have to!" and then lay flat on the floor. At least two adults were always required to remove him.

Dameon thought the block area was his. He didn't see that other children might share his desire to play with the blocks.

I talked with the preschool teachers, and we decided not to remove him from the block area when he threw blocks. Instead, we used the following strategies:

- When Dameon built his tall building, he would use masking tape and place it on the carpeting around his structure. This gave him ownership of his space and let others know to avoid it unless they were invited.

- When other children entered the block area, we asked Dameon to show them what he built. He could decide whether the other children could be part of his activity or if they needed to build on their own.

- If Dameon chose not to have the other children participate in his building structure, we made sure he knew that their building was going to occur in a different location.

Dameon not only stopped throwing blocks—he invited other children to be involved in his building. Dameon needed to feel a sense of power, which is difficult for some boys to experience in a group setting. Granting him ownership of his building activity helped him to see that sharing a space does not mean losing control. This provided Dameon with the power that he really needed. Within weeks, Dameon was asking children to join him in his building. Had we continued removing him from the block area, he would have lost the opportunity to change into the caring and cooperative child he became.

Ralph the "runner"

At age four, Ralph attended preschool three mornings a week. Each day he came into the center and ran toward the "large motor" area. When he got to that center he would run, and he did not stop until it was time to go home.

His parents were concerned. They asked the preschool teacher if he was ever going to "settle down," become less active, and read or complete another quiet task. I was called in to observe his behavior and see how I might help.

Ralph definitely did run during preschool, and he did so as often as he could. Yet I came to understand that the running wasn't the problem. The real issue was the lack of enticements for him to do anything *other* than running. During a meeting with the preschool staff, we decided to move some books and some writing tools into the large motor area.

The next time Ralph came to preschool, he again ran to the large motor area and started running. While he did this, I sat down in the same area with a book. Within minutes, Ralph moved towards me and started to look at the book I was reading. I asked him, "Is this a book you might like me to read to you?" Ralph said, "Yes" and sat down beside me. He listened to that book and then asked for another to be read.

Putting activities in the large motor area that enticed him motivated Ralph to expand his experiences. His running wasn't bad. We just opened his eyes to other experiences that he might enjoy as well. Based on this experience, the other adults in that preschool began to look at how they might integrate other activities in various locations.

Putting yourself in a boy's place

Every morning the children arrived at preschool and I greeted them at the door with, "Good morning, I have been waiting for you!" One morning Arick arrived and I greeted him, "Arick, I have been waiting for you!"

Arick looked at me with his mischievous smile and asked, "How long would you wait?"

"Arick," I replied, "for you I would wait forever!"

He smiled and jumped over to his favorite place, the block area.

Boys need a teacher who is waiting for them. Yet many boys get exactly the opposite message from their teachers: *How long will it take for you to change into the child I want you to be?*

One morning in my preschool classroom, I could hear the repeated flushing of a toilet. Concerned, I went to the bathroom, knocked on the door and announced, "It's Dan. Can I come in?"

Arick, from inside the bathroom responded, "Sure, come on in." When I went inside I saw that Arick had two shoes and socks off, standing inside the toilet bowl, flushing repeatedly, with a big smile on his face. I panicked and took Arick out of the toilet bowl, washed his feet off, and said to him, "You cannot put your feet in the toilet, but I will find something for you to put your feet in when we get into the classroom."

Arick and I walked into the classroom and I took off his shoes and socks, put water in a small tub and gave him an eggbeater to churn the water with.

I asked Arick, "Does that feel good?"

Arick responded, "Yes" and smiled.

Wow, I thought, *I solved the problem without too much disturbance.*

The very next day in the preschool classroom, I again heard the repeated flushing of a toilet. Concerned, I went to the bathroom and knocked on the door again.

"It's Dan. Can I come in?"

Two voices answered this time. Arick and Michael said, "Come on in."

When I went inside, I saw that Arick had one shoe off and Michael had one shoe off and they were sharing the toilet bowl as they took turns flushing. This time I did not panic. I simply said, "I can tell by your smiles that this must feel real good."

Arick and Michael laughed. "It does, Dan, and you try it!"

I paused for a moment and then went over to the toilet bowl. By then Arick and Michael had jumped out, watching what I was going to do with wide-open eyes.

I took one shoe and sock off, looked down in the toilet bowl (which is very important) and put my foot into it. "Give it a flush," I told Arick and Michael.

I am here to tell you that it felt wonderful. It was like a cold whirlpool for my foot. I now knew I was in real trouble. How could I tell Arick and Michael not to do something that felt that good?

I took my foot out, and the boys and I washed our feet. Then we knelt down on the floor, looking at the toilet bowl.

"I know that putting your feet into the toilet felt good, but I can't let you continue with that game," I said to Arick and Michael. "I am afraid that your foot will get stuck in that small hole and I might not be able to get you out."

They nodded their heads in agreement.

We went back to the classroom and found some more tubs, into which I poured water. For days they used the tubs along with eggbeaters to create the same feeling they had enjoyed with their feet in the toilet bowl.

What is the moral of this story? It is that sometimes we need to put ourselves in a child's place to really understand what and why they do what they do. Boys are looking for a chance to grow and develop. Our job as teachers is to look at the research and now put it to practice.

WHAT BOYS NEED?	
Movable Parts	Lots of Space
Running	Climbing
Capes	Writing on the Go!
Less Talking	Digging
Visual Clues	Rough & Tumble Play
Louder Voices	Time to Solve
Books on the Go!	Visual Boundaries
Boxes for Kicking	More Male Teachers

6 Conclusion

I hope this book helps you look deeper into the understanding of how boys' brains are wired differently then girls. Boys are counting on us to create environments supported by directors, teachers, parents and communities that create avenues of belonging.

Children develop a sense of belonging when their needs for hunger are addressed, when their needs for touch are addressed, and when adults respond to their emotional needs.

Boys are looking for that sense of belonging. If they do not get a feeling of belonging from their family they look for it at school. If they don't get it at school, they look for it in the community. If they don't get it in any of those places, they have no choice but to create it. That is often called "gangs."

As early childhood professionals we can prevent the growth of gangs from happening. Just make changes that create boy-enriched environments, such as:

- Climbing
- Moveable parts
- Tools rather than toys
- More time to play
- Adults who ask, "What do you need?"
- Running
- Roughhousing
- Allowing louder voices

Parents and educators are taking a hard look at boys. They wonder what is causing the gender gap in our educational system. They want to know why boys fail.

It is time for us to revisit what we think and what we know about boys. It is time to relearn. In part, this means recognizing and respecting the reality that boys and girls are different, that each gender has distinct needs and distinct strengths. If we fail to do this, we will create problems for early childhood professionals and for our children.

Boys need to hear that demonstrating

their feelings in actions rather than words is normal, natural, and good.

Boys want to know that the need to be active isn't wrong—it is necessary.

Boys need to learn by recognizing that taking more time and repeating tasks makes them more successful.

Boys need to be convinced that their strengths and their vulnerabilities should be celebrated.

If we are willing to transform our early childhood settings, our children will become capable of growth that we have not yet imagined. Boys and girls will be allowed to explore their individuality in a variety of exciting ways. Children work hard at understanding their gender. And they will express that understanding fearlessly, with intelligence and love.

I am counting on you to join me in this effort. Working together, we can give boys and girls the strength and creativity they need to face the future and master their changing world.

Resources

Boss, Bev. (2001) *Together We're Better.* Turn the Page Press

Boss, Bev, and Jenny Chapman. (2006) *Tumbling Over the Edge.* Turn the Page Press

Clare, Cherry. (1982) *Please Don't Sit on the Kids.* Fearon Early Childhood Library

Fox, Mem. (1993) *Radical Reflections on Teaching, Learning and Living.* Harcourt Inc.

Garbarino, James. (1999) *Lost Boys.* Free Press

Gurian, Michael (2001) *Boys and Girls Learn Differently.* Jossey-Boss

Gurian, Michael. (2004) *The Wonder of Boys.* Jossey-Boss

Healy, Jane. (1999) *Failure to Connect: How Computers affect our children's minds and what we can do about it.* Simon & Schuster

Kohn, Alfie. (1999) *The Schools Our Children Deserve.* Houghton Mifflin

Moir, Anne and Jessel, David. (1991) *Brain Sex.* Dell

Moir, Anne and Moir Bill. (1999) *Why Men Don't Iron.* Citadel Press

Paley, Vivian. (1984) *Boys and Girls Superheros in the Doll Corner.* Chicago Press

Pollack, William. (1998) *Real Boys.* Henry Holt

Sommers, Christina Hoff. (2006) *The War Against Boys.* Touchstone

Tyre, Peg. (2008) *The Trouble With Boys.* Crown Publishing Group

Category Index

A

Active play 26
Allow for choice and change 40
Arick the "hitter" 91
Art comes from the inside 41

B

Beliefs and practices 24
Books and boys 60
Boyhood in our culture 13
Boys' developmental age can differ from their chronological age 8
Boys are wired for assertiveness 12
Boys experience sensory overload 10
Boys go into "pause state" after completing tasks 1
Boys in groups focus on tasks rather than process 19
Boys in groups work out codes 18
Boys in trouble vii
Boys process feelings differently than girls 3
Boys see the whole more than the details 6

C

Center subject choices 62
Climbing spaces 30
Computers and boys—early isn't always better 70
Criteria for selecting books for boys 64

D

Dameon the "bomber" 92
Digging spaces 33

E

Effective responses 75
Environment, the 25

H

How can I avoid getting into power struggles with boys? 78
How can I deal with roughhousing? 80
How can I get aggressive boys to stop hitting? 76
How can I help boys develop healthy emotional bonds? 86
How can I help boys listen more effectively? 85
How can I model effective behavior for boys? 73
How can I respond to boys who use loud voices? 84

I

Invitations we send 26
Is the time-out chair an effective strategy for boys? 80

L

Letter to parents 15
Let children drive the curriculum 40